Caribbean Examinations Cou

Economics

CAPE

CXC®

UNIT 1

for self-study and distance learning

OXFORD
UNIVERSITY PRESS

Great Clarendon Street, Oxford, OX2 6DP, United Kingdom

Oxford University Press is a department of the University of Oxford.
It furthers the University's objective of excellence in research, scholarship,
and education by publishing worldwide. Oxford is a registered trade mark of
Oxford University Press in the UK and in certain other countries

First published by the Caribbean Examinations Council in association
with The Commonwealth of Learning in 2006
Second edition repackaged and distributed by Nelson Thornes Ltd in 2011
This edition distributed by Oxford University Press in 2015

British Library Cataloguing in Publication Data
Data available

978-1-4085-0907-4

10 9 8 7 6 5

Printed and bound by CPI Group (UK) Ltd, Croydon, CR0 4YY

Acknowledgements

Cover image: Mark Lyndersay, Lyndersay Digital, Trinidad, (www.lyndersaydigital.com)
Page make-up: The OKS Group

Caribbean Examinations Council/Oxford University Press would like to acknowledge
Roger Hosein and Rebecca Gookool for their assistance in preparing the content
for this Self-Study Guide.

Contents

Introduction

Purpose

The Caribbean Examinations Council (CXC®) has developed Self-Study Guides for a number of Caribbean Secondary Education Certificate (CSEC®) and Caribbean Advanced Proficiency Examination (CAPE®) subjects. The main purpose of the guides is to provide both in-school and out-of-school candidates with resource materials that should help them in preparing for CXC examinations. Each Study Guide is student-centred and its language is student-friendly.

This course is designed for persons over the age of 16 who wish to further their studies. The course is equally useful to persons who are pursuing part-time study and those enrolled full time in an educational institution.

You may have completed five years of secondary education, or you may be a mature student with work experience. The course is based on the assumption that you already have a good grasp of the Caribbean Secondary Education Certificate (CSEC) Economics syllabus or its equivalent.

Course aims

The course aims to:

- promote understanding of the basic principles and concepts of economics that are accepted in large measure by economists while recognising that the field is changing continuously
- help students to develop an appreciation of the various methods used by economists in analysing economic problems
- develop students' understanding of the global economy and of the relationships between rich and poor nations with respect to international trade and finance and the most important international financial institutions
- encourage students to apply economic principles, theories and tools to everyday economic problems, for example, inflation, unemployment, environmental degradation and exchange rate instability, and to contribute meaningfully to any dialogue on these issues
- encourage students to apply economic theory to the critical issues that affect the small open Caribbean-type economy
- encourage students to evaluate contentious economic issues so that decision-making may be informed by logical thinking.

Course structure

The course comprises 10 chapters which are all based on Unit 1 of the CAPE Economics Syllabus. Each chapter addresses the skills and content of a specific Module of the syllabus. The sequence of the chapters mirrors that of the syllabus Modules to a large extent, except for those topics that span more than one Module. The sequence of topics in this course is designed to facilitate study by leading you through topics in a way that will enable you to build on previously learnt skills.

What resources will you need?

Remember that this Study Guide will not be all that you need to complete the syllabus and prepare for your examination. You are expected to engage in other wide general reading, which will improve your general knowledge and vocabulary.

You will also need basic study equipment, for example, paper, pens, pencils and highlighters, for marking important parts of the text.

Managing your time

Remember to put aside a special time each day for general reading in addition to your study time.

Study Guide structure

The Study Guide is structured to facilitate your study, as follows.

Content   This lists the topics that are covered in the chapter.

Objectives   These help you to identify the specific skills that you should have acquired by the end of the Module and the chapter. You should read these carefully to acquaint yourself with what you are meant to be learning during the section.

Examples   These are meant to guide you to an understanding of the concept being taught. All examples should be read carefully before you attempt any activities that follow.

Activities	Instructions are provided at the start of each activity. Read all instructions carefully before you attempt the activity.
Feedback	Each activity has feedback that allows you to determine how well you have done in the activity. If you have not completed the activity successfully you should re-read the preceding examples or information carefully.
Key points	These summarise important concepts that you need to remember and pay special attention to in the future.
End test	This comes at the end of each Module and is designed to ensure that you have acquired those skills identified in the objectives. There is feedback following the End test that allows you to measure the accuracy of your answers to the test so that you will know whether or not you have acquired the competencies. If

there are questions in the End test that you have not answered satisfactorily, ensure that you return to the relevant section of the Module and review those areas until you are satisfied that you have understood the concept.

Assignments

Course assignments are included in order to allow you to check your progress through the course. The assignments enable you to determine your areas of weakness and to check your understanding of the concepts.

Examination

Please refer to the latest syllabus for guidance on the structure of the exam, the number of papers, the length of each paper, what marks are allocated to each question and the structure of the school-based assessment.

1

Module 1: Methodology demand and supply
The central problem of economics

Content

- The meaning of scarcity, free goods and economic goods
- The concept of opportunity cost
  - Definition of opportunity cost
  - Choice: what, how and for whom to produce
  - The concept of opportunity cost applied to economic agents (individuals, households, firms and governments)
- Production possibility frontiers
  - Assumptions: maximum output attainable, given full employment and constant state of technology
  - Regions: attainable, unattainable, efficient and inefficient levels of production
- Production possibilities frontier: slopes and shapes
- Use of production possibilities frontier to show growth and technological change
- Examples of positive and normative statements
- Different types of economic systems: traditional, market, planned and mixed

Scarcity

Scarcity, referred to as the central problem of economics, implies that there are not enough resources to meet the needs of all economic agents. In such an environment it is therefore necessary to make choices. Choices are made at every level of the economy; at the level of the individual and the firm (the micro level) as well as at the level of the entire economy (the macro level).

In the micro-economy, consumers make choices about what goods and services to purchase in their everyday lives. In the productive sector, firms have to make decisions on how to distribute scarce resources among those inputs needed for their production operations, namely those factors of production consisting of land, labour, capital and entrepreneurial talent. At the economy-wide level choices are made regarding what to produce, how to go about producing and for whom to produce.

Figure 1.1 on the following page describes the relationships among wants and needs and the means to achieving those needs. Specifically, it shows that scarce resources in the context of infinite wants will force users of goods and services, both at the micro- and macroeconomic levels to make these choices.

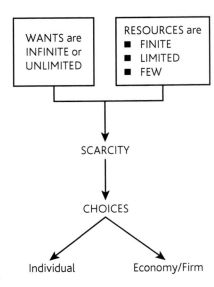

Figure 1.1 *Relationship between needs, wants and limited resources*

Example

Opportunity cost to the consumer

Jayelle has a fixed allowance of $100.00 per week. She is faced with several competing uses for her money. She wants to buy snacks, go to the movies and photocopy past examination papers. Since $100.00 will not satisfy all of her wants, Jayelle is forced to make choices, fully aware that she must prioritise her wants.

If Jayelle decides to use the $100.00 for movies and snacks, then the photocopying of examination past papers is her opportunity cost.

Free goods and economic goods

A free good in economics is a good or service for which the opportunity cost of consumption to society is zero. In other words, the commodity is not scarce in relation to demand. However, it should be noted that a good that is offered free of charge is not necessarily a 'free good' in the pure economic sense, in that scarce resources are utilised in the production of that commodity.

According to economic literature there are essentially two categories of free goods: goods that are supplied abundantly by nature such as air; and goods that are produced as by-products of others, such as red mud from the processing of bauxite.

An economic good refers to a good or service that is valued by individuals and thus can be sold at a non-negative price in the market. These goods are relatively scarce in supply in relation to demand for them at zero prices. Thus, when these goods are consumed, an opportunity cost is involved.

Opportunity cost

When any economic agent makes a choice among competing alternatives, an opportunity cost is incurred. In economics the concept of cost is quite different from that in accounting, in that the accountant measures cost in terms of dollars and cents, while economists measure costs in terms of what is given up, or the sacrifice of one option for another. This type of cost is called opportunity cost.

In economics we use the term 'opportunity cost' to refer to the cost of one choice in terms of the next best alternative. The concept of opportunity cost can be applied at individual, household, firm and government levels. For example, at the individual level the opportunity cost of doing CAPE Economics is the income that a student may have earned in that time period if they opted to get a job. At the household level, the opportunity cost of purchasing a new vehicle is the vacation they may have given up.

Firms are constantly trying to maximise profits by making the best choices possible given the factors of production at their disposal. For example, the opportunity cost of installing new machinery would be the expansion in the recreation facility for employees that was forfeited.

At a government level, one can say that the opportunity cost of a government's decision to expand the local hospital is the expansion in the primary schools that would have been funded by the same resources.

Altogether then, opportunity cost refers to the benefits of the next best alternative that is given up for what was chosen. The concept of opportunity cost therefore assumes that the economic agent ranks the alternative choices available to them; in other words the consumer prioritises the alternatives along a scale of preference.

One of the main tools used to analyse the choices made by firms, or even economies, is the production possibility frontier (PPF).

Production possibility frontier (PPF)

The PPF is a macroeconomic tool that represents the point at which an economy is most efficiently producing its goods and services and, therefore, allocating its resources in the best way possible. If the firm or the economy is not producing the quantities indicated along the boundary of the PPF, resources are being managed inefficiently and the output produced is less than optimal.

The production possibility curve, or the production possibility boundary, shows that there are limits to production for the firm or the economy being considered. It should be noted, however, that several assumptions are made in constructing production possibility curves or boundaries. The assumptions made include the following:

- Two goods: the assumption of two goods (or services or groups of goods and services) allows us to graphically illustrate the trade-offs in production or the opportunity cost involved in differing production levels.
- Common resources: this implies that the same factors of production (though in differing combinations) are used to produce either of the two goods.
- Fixed resources: the quantity of factors of production is assumed to be fixed. This assumption disqualifies the possibility of increasing the production of one good without reducing the production of the other, given full employment of factors of production. Points along the boundary of the PPF represent full employment of factors of production.
- Fixed technology: this assumption is made in order to disqualify the possibility of increasing the production of one good without having the production of the other falling given full employment of factors of production.

Figure 1.2 shows the PPF for a given firm.

Let us assume that this firm can use its resources to produce two goods, clothing (X) and food (Y). The firm can produce y_5 units of Y and 0 units of X, or x_5 units of X and 0 units of Y, or any combination of X and Y along the curve itself.

Because the firm has a limited amount of scarce resources it cannot produce at point D. D is therefore unattainable. This point is reflective of the concept of scarcity. At the same time, while the economy can easily produce at C it is very much within the boundaries of the production possibility curve. Point C represents an inefficient yet attainable production point as some of its resources would remain idle or unemployed.

> ## Activity 1.1
> Select the opportunity cost in the following scenarios.
>
> 1 Jayelle has money to buy a pair of sneakers or an economics textbook. She chooses the pair of sneakers.
>
> 2 Amartya chooses to do her homework instead of going to the party.
>
> 3 Daniel gives a donation to the church. He could have used the money to visit New York.
>
> 4 Stephen pays for guitar lessons. He could have taken his girlfriend on a date.
>
> *Feedback*
> _____
>
> 1 The economics textbook.
> 2 Attending the party.
> 3 The visit to New York.
> 4 The date with his girlfriend.
> _____

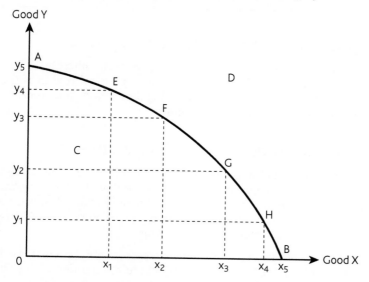

Figure 1.2 *Production possibility frontier*

Note that this firm can choose to operate anywhere within or on the production possibility curve. Thus, at point E the firm can produce y_4 units of Y and x_1 units of X, while at point F the firm can produce y_3 units of Y and x_2 units of X, and so on. It can be said that the combinations on the PPF itself are Pareto optimal in that, for the output of one of the commodities in the combination to increase, output of the other commodity must fall. This is implicit in the shape of the curve itself.

Activity 1.2

This activity will help you determine opportunity cost.

Using Figure 1.2, explain the opportunity cost in the following cases. The first one is done for you.

1 The firm was originally producing at Point E but shifts its production to Point F.

Answer: Assuming that X = clothing and Y = food, at point E the firm was producing one unit of clothing (x_1) and four units of food (y_4).

By shifting to point F, the firm is now producing two units of clothing (x_2) and three units of food (y_3). The firm has therefore given up one unit of food (y_4 to y_3) to produce the extra unit of clothing (x_1 to x_2). The opportunity cost therefore, defined as what is given up or sacrificed, is one unit of food (y_1).

2 What is the opportunity cost if the firm shifts production from point E to point G?

3 What is the opportunity cost if the firm shifts production from point E to point H?

4 What is the opportunity cost if the firm shifts production from point G to point F?

5 What is the opportunity cost if the firm shifts production from point G to point H?

6 What is the opportunity cost if the firm shifts production from point E to point H?

7 What is the opportunity cost if the firm shifts production from point C to point E?

Feedback

---

2 y_4 to y_2

3 y_4 to y_1

4 x_3 to x_2

5 y_2 to y_1

6 y_4 to y_1

7 0. The firm does not have to give up any of the two goods.

Marginal rate of transformation

Opportunity cost is measured as a slope between two alternative combinations, for example from E to F. The slope is referred to as the marginal rate of transformation (MRT). Figure 1.2 is an illustration of a typical PPF that is concave to the origin.

Shifts in the production possibility curve

An outward movement of the production possibility curve indicates that the firm's productive capacity has expanded, or that the economy has benefited from economic growth. This is shown in Figure 1.3. A number of factors can lead to an outward shift in the production possibility of a firm or an economy, including the following:

- Investment inflows: as investment increases there is an increase in the stock of capital, both in the firm and in the economy. This will result in an overall increase in the output of all commodities.

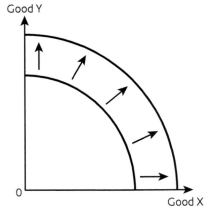

Figure 1.3 *Expansion of the PPF*

- Expansion of human resources and human capital: as the quality and quantity of people in the firm or in an economy increases the productive capacity at either the firm or economy level will expand. An increase in the size of the labour force will lead to an increase in the amount of factors of production that can contribute to the productive process. This would cause a rightward shift of the PPF. An increase in the quality of the labour force, on the other hand, would result in the increase in the productivity of the labour force, the result of which would be the same as if the labour force increased quantitatively.

- Technical/technological change: an improvement in the quality of the technology utilised in an economy usually translates that all factors of production can now offer a higher level of output with the implication that the PPF shifts rightwards.

- Competition: in a free enterprise economy there is rigorous competition among firms. This competition fosters efficiency as firms adopt improved techniques in production and produce better-quality products. This leads to an expansion of productive output in various sectors of the economy via the capital stock and the level of technology employed. These factors cause an outward shift in the PPF, as growth and national development is achieved.

- Resource boom: as a result of the crude oil/natural gas boom, such as in Trinidad and Tobago, the nation is able to produce and export a greater quantity of those commodities.

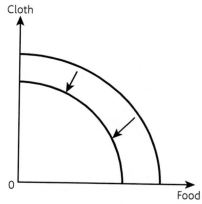

Figure 1.4 *Economic contraction*

Productive/economic contraction

Figure 1.4 shows that the overall level of output produced by either the firm or the economy falls. At the firm level as well as at the economy level, several factors can be responsible for this, including the reduction in the quantity or quality of the factors of production employed.

At the macroeconomic level there are some changes that may initiate an economic contraction. They include the following.

Coup d'état

A coup d'état is evidence of political and social unrest within an economy. A coup d'état has the effect of reducing investor confidence in the economy and, as such, both local and foreign investment can possibly fall. A coup d'état also has the negative effect of driving the existing foreign investors out of the economy. Falling investment levels have the macroeconomic effect of constraining economic growth and development and so compromise the growth of the economy.

Example
Crime in Trinidad and Tobago

Trinidad and Tobago had the unfortunate experience of political unrest in July 1990. This experience left the streets of the capital city, Port of Spain, in shambles. The militant group responsible, the Jamaat al Muslimeen, held the country to ransom for six days during which time they occupied the Parliament. During this time the then Prime Minister, the Hon. A. N. R. Robinson, was shot in the leg. Law and order was eventually restored by the Trinidad and Tobago regiment. This attempted coup had a relatively devastating effect on the economy over the following months in terms of loss of consumer confidence in the political sovereignty of the state.

Natural disasters

Natural disasters such as hurricanes or earthquakes have the devastating effect of destroying both the physical and natural infrastructure of a country. One example is that of hurricane Ivan and the extent of devastation caused in Grenada in September of 2004. This disaster crippled the Grenadian economy to the extent that almost one year after the hurricane the economy was still struggling to recover.

Example

Hurricane Ivan: devastation in Grenada

In September 2004 Hurricane Ivan devastated up to 85 per cent of the small island state of Grenada. Twenty-nine people were killed and a substantial amount of the island's physical infrastructure was destroyed. The Grenadian economy was severely crippled in terms of its own growth potential, in that prior to the hurricane the estimated growth of the economy over the period 2005 to 2007 was expected to be 5 per cent, but as a result of the hurricane this estimate was reduced to less than 1 per cent.

As it stands, government debt has also increased substantially.

A more recent example is the experience of the citizens of New Orleans who faced the full force of hurricane Katrina. As an application exercise, what do you think the economic effects of the hurricane would be for the US economy? Consider the example on the right.

Example

Hurricane Katrina: New Orleans

Hurricane Katrina was the eleventh hurricane of the 2005 Atlantic hurricane season. It hit near New Orleans, Louisiana, on 29 August 2005 and its storm torrent breached the levees that protected New Orleans from Lake Pontchartrain. As a result, the Lake's waters flooded most of the city. This, along with major damage to the Louisiana, Mississippi and Alabama coastal regions, made Katrina the most destructive and costliest tropical cyclone ever to hit the US.

Hurricane Katrina has already had devastating economic effects that are expected to continue into the long term. Experts predicted that Katrina would be the most expensive natural disaster in US history, exceeding that of hurricane Andrew. Early estimates of damage done by the hurricane exceeded US$200bn. This did not include the potential detrimental inland damage due to the flooding or the negative economic effects caused by potential obstruction of the oil supply and exports of commodities such as grain.

In addition, the region had previously supported about one million non-farm jobs, 600,000 of them in New Orleans, before the hurricane hit. These people were thus displaced, causing a humanitarian crisis on a scale unmatched in the US since the San Francisco earthquake of 1906.

Health risks and the quality of the labour force

The HIV/AIDS pandemic has so adversely affected the labour force in parts of the world that production has slowed to a grinding halt in some places, for example Chad and Somalia. As it stands, the statistics show that the Caribbean as a region ranks second only to sub-Saharan Africa. Trinidad and Tobago ranks as one of the countries with highest per capita incidence of HIV/AIDS in the region. Jamaica and Haiti also rank high on the list.

HIV/AIDS has an adverse effect on the labour force in that this disease effectively reduces the productive life of labour by reducing the amount of productive days per unit of labour. An HIV/AIDS-ridden population will result in an HIV/AIDS-ridden labour force which will be essentially unproductive. This will also have a negative implication on the future generations, which may be more susceptible to this disease as well as others. It is therefore necessary to consider the implication of HIV/AIDS, especially in terms of manpower planning, due to the fact that the age group with highest incidence of infection is the 19–45 age group, which makes up a significant portion of the labour force.

Example

HIV/AIDS and the labour force

By the end of 2003, it was estimated that half a million persons were living with HIV/AIDS in the Caribbean, and an average of 50,000 new persons were being infected annually, a significant portion of which were women. In 2003 alone, the estimated number of deaths from the disease was 35,000. On the basis of these statistics it is reasonable to assume that the impact on the labour force is substantial or rather has the potential to seriously adversely affect the productive capacity of an economy.

Labour is a factor of production, and, as such, changes to the quantity and/or quality of that factor of production will affect the capacity and capability of an economy to produce output. As such the threat of HIV/AIDS must not be taken lightly.

Crime and migration

Criminal activity has the adverse impact of reducing investor confidence in the business aspects of the economy, with the effect of diverting funds away from the local economy. Crime also has the effect of discouraging persons from remaining in the country; therefore crime may cause excessive migration. The issue of crime has been a key social and political focal point of discussion in Caribbean economies, due especially to the upsurge in the number and incidence of kidnapping taking place in Trinidad and Tobago. Other types of criminal activity have also been on the increase on the islands, including murders, the toll for which, as at the middle of 2005, was over 250.

Example

Crime waves in Jamaica and Trinidad and Tobago

In recent years, murders in Jamaica and kidnappings in Trinidad and Tobago have become major social problems. According to the *Los Angeles Times* (January 2005), there were fewer than 10 kidnappings in Trinidad and Tobago in 2001, in 2002 it had increased to 29 and from 2003 to 2004 the figure skyrocketed to 150.

The rate of kidnappings in Trinidad and Tobago and murders in Jamaica have reached a level where affluent business persons are seriously considering migrating as an option to reduce the risk of becoming victims.

Distortions in factor markets

If the markets for factors of production such as labour and capital do not function efficiently, this may lead to inefficient allocation of resources in an economy. This can result in a fall in its achievable output and thus an inward shift of the production possibility curve.

For example, the structural problems that Japan's factor markets faced resulted in economic stagnation in the 1990s. Therefore, measures must be taken to achieve a more efficient allocation of productive resources.

Types of opportunity cost

Some production possibility curves are convex to the origin, in which case the slope decreases from left to right along the curve. This is reflective of decreasing opportunity cost, while other production possibility curves that are represented by a straight line have constant gradients and are reflective of constant opportunity costs. Some PPFs may also have an increasing gradient. Further explanations and diagrammatic representations are given on the following pages.

Constant opportunity cost

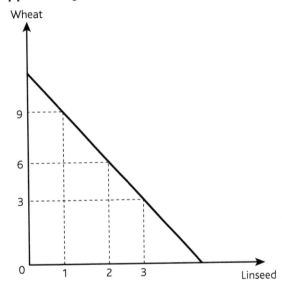

Figure 1.5 *PPF showing constant opportunity cost*

A production possibility curve that takes a linear form illustrates constant returns or constant opportunity cost. This implies that for every consecutive increase in the production of one commodity, an equal amount of the other is given up every time. For example, the firm may produce one unit of linseed and nine units of wheat. If it wishes to increase production of linseed to two units, three units of wheat are sacrificed. If three units of linseed are produced, three units of wheat must again be sacrificed. Thus, the opportunity cost or the returns would remain constant, at three units of wheat for every unit of linseed produced, over the entire PPF. The marginal rate of substitution is also constant at every point along the PPF. Producers that have the same production processes and use similar factors of production will therefore have a PPF exhibiting constant opportunity cost.

Decreasing opportunity cost and increasing returns

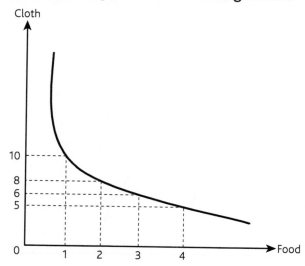

Figure 1.6 *PPF showing decreasing opportunity cost*

In Figure 1.6, the production possibility curve has a continually decreasing slope. In this case, for every consecutive increase in the production of one commodity, less and less of the other is given up. This diagram shows decreasing opportunity cost or increasing returns.

Increasing opportunity cost and decreasing returns

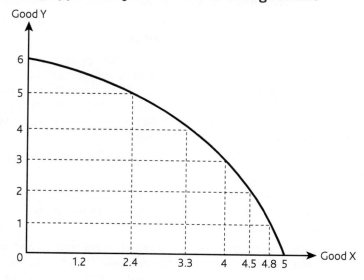

Figure 1.7 *PPF showing increasing opportunity cost*

In Figure 1.7, when 5 units of good X are being produced 0 units of good Y are produced. In order to get the first unit of Y, 0.2 units of good X has to be given up. To get the second unit of Y, 0.3 units of good X has to be given up. The opportunity cost keeps increasing as shown in the Figure above. This type of PPF shows increasing opportunity cost and is concave to the origin. Decreasing returns are exhibited because it becomes more difficult or expensive to switch resources for the production of one good (say good X) to the production of the other good (say good Y) since they require types of different resources.

Change in slope

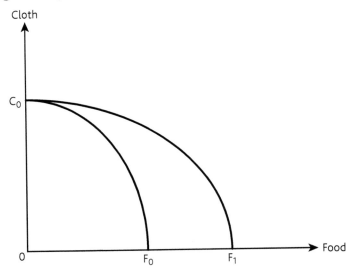

Figure 1.8 *Improvement in the factor of production most used to produce food*

If there is an increase (quantity or quality) in a factor of production that is biased towards the output of one set of goods only, then the PPF would change slope. So, let us assume that food is a labour-intensive commodity, that is, food production uses a relatively high amount of labour as compared to cloth; in which case an inflow of labour can change the slope of the PPF from C_0F_0 to C_0F_1.

Positive and normative economics

Positive statements address matters of fact. As such, positive statements are objective statements and made without value judgements, opinions or emotions. As an extension of this line of reasoning, therefore, positive economics is concerned with the facts of 'what is, what was and what will be'. Positive economics therefore can be tested. Some examples of positive economic statements include the following:

- An increase in the rate of interest will result in an increase in the exchange rate.
- Lowering income tax will positively affect consumer spending.
- As market prices for tomatoes fall, the quantity of tomatoes demanded will increase.

Normative statements on the other hand are based on opinion and are not often premised on sound theory. They are value judgements and are concerned with 'what ought to be'. Normative statements cannot be tested. Some examples of normative statements in economics include the following:

- The minimum wage is undesirable as it results in higher unemployment and inflation rates.
- The only way to improve living standards is to impose protectionist policies.
- Poverty is always linked to criminal behaviour.

Economic systems: alternative methods of allocation

An economic system refers to the network of economic agents whose interaction is geared towards answering the fundamental allocation problems of what to produce, how to produce and for whom to produce. Essentially, economic systems are organised into four broad categories:

- traditional economy
- planned, command, communist and totalitarian economy
- free-economy market
- mixed economy

An in-depth discussion into the description and explanation of each market type will now be presented.

Traditional economy

A traditional economy is one that is based on customs and traditions. All allocation decisions regarding the fundamental economic questions of *what to produce*, *how to produce* and *for whom to produce* are determined by cultural norms and traditions. One of the closest examples of such a society in today's modern world is that of the Inuit tribes of the Arctic.

Planned, command, communist and totalitarian economies

In a command economy the majority of decision-making is undertaken by a central planning authority. Both the price and quantity of any good that is produced is determined by the government. Each firm has production quotas on the amount of output it produces. The central planning authority also directs resource movement and so directs the amount of resources to each productive enterprise. In a centrally planned economy the central planning authority perceives that it has the most optimal resource-allocating capabilities in the economy.

Although in a centrally planned economic system consumers still have their preference rankings, the state governs the resource allocation process. In a centrally planned economy only a small amount of the decision-making is made by the private sector. In this type of economic system the overall level of efficiency is conditioned on how accurately the central planning authority forecasts future demand and supply. In many cases the output mix that the economy produces may be inefficient, as the price of frequently used consumer goods may be set very low as compared to what would have prevailed in the free market. An example of a planned economy in the region is the Cuban economy.

Advantages of the planned economy

In a centrally planned economy factors of production and property are owned collectively by the citizens of the nation. Thus, the economy operates without the price mechanism that generates market prices and profits. This price mechanism is incentive-driven and creates productive activity. However, advocates of the centrally planned system argue that these incentives do not matter and thus there is no need for such a mechanism to exist.

Command-type economies are usually characterised by equality and equity in the distribution of income and goods and services.

Disadvantages of the command-type system for allocating scarce resources

The state frequently encourages an output mix of commodities that is different from those desired by households. If prices are set above the free-market price, that is, if prices are set at very high levels, then large surpluses may develop in the economy, for example, beef mountains.

In the command economy there is a high degree of planning by all levels of government in order to allocate resources. Large amounts of labour resources are often used inefficiently and wastefully in this process.

The coordinating and controlling of these plans also tend to be very difficult. This results from the sheer size of the projects undertaken for the entire economy, as well as the complex 'matching' of actual production with consumer demand. This system also can be prone to a high degree of corruption as there are few decision-makers responsible for resource allocation.

The absence of healthy competition in command economies may result in productive and allocative inefficiencies. This relates to several issues such as ineffective methods of production, high costs of production and goods that are low in quality and limited in variety for the consumer.

Free-market economies

The free market represents the other side of the spectrum as concerns economic systems governing the allocation of scarce resources. In the free market, private economic agents pursuing their own self-interest are responsible for the allocation of scarce resources. In this type of economic system there is a very limited role for the state in allocating scarce economic resources and in fact its prime task is to produce an environment for the free market to operate properly, for example, it provides national security services, a Bureau of Standards.

In the free-market economy, prices act as a signal to both producers and consumers. When the price for a commodity is low, consumers will move resources into purchasing that commodity, and when a commodity's price is high, consumers will move resources towards relatively cheaper commodities. As concerns firms, when prices are relatively low, firms will move resources out of that product into other areas where prices are relatively higher. Prices therefore provide a signal regarding what and how much of a good firms should produce to optimise their profits. At the same time these prices provide a signal to consumers regarding how much they should purchase to maximise their welfare. By operating in this way, the price mechanism helps to ensure that resources are efficiently allocated.

In the free-market system, prices, output levels and the allocation of scarce resources are determined by the price mechanism.

Advantages of the free market

In a free-market system there is freedom of choice, both at the individual as well as at the firm level. Individuals make their own decisions about what to buy, while firms and businessmen alike are free to produce.

In a free-market or capitalist system, economic entities are free to acquire and own property and other types of assets.

The free-market system is efficient in terms of the fact that the price mechanism allocates resources according to its most profitable uses.

Prices are determined by the market mechanism, that is, forces of demand and supply. In this type of system prices act as feedback to signal the changes in the market conditions.

Disadvantages of the free market

In the free-market economy it is possible that the emergent distribution of income could be very unequal, so that some economic agents own a vast amount of wealth alongside others who own very little.

At prevailing market prices, those economic agents without the appropriate levels of income might not be able to afford basic economic goods necessary for living.

The price mechanism underproduces some goods and overproduces others. For example, the market produces too few seat belts or sugar-free drinks, too many cigarettes and too much alcohol.

In the free-market system, competition can allow the most efficient firm to eventually dominate the market and become a monopoly. Acting as a monopolist, however, the firm will produce too low an output and sell at too high a price as compared to a firm operating in an intensely competitive environment.

Because ability to pay strongly influences the type of goods produced, a production pattern skewed in favour of the type of goods required by the rich can result in a free-market economy.

Mixed economies

In a mixed economy some decisions are made by the state and some by the private sector. Mixed economies have emerged to help bridge some of the problems that emerge with pure free-market economies. They provide a basis for some degree of government involvement in a free economy.

Characteristics of the mixed economy

Both the government and the private sector are involved in the production of goods and services.

There is some degree of regulation of the market mechanism to reduce the degree of inequity and the extent of externalities that may be created if the system is left to market forces.

The government regulates prices to the extent that they are not exploitative of consumers. In this regard some of the price controls include price ceilings and price floors.

Conclusion

This chapter considered the concepts of scarcity, choice and opportunity costs with real-life applications. Additionally the concept of production possibility curves was considered. The PPF was used to illustrate constant returns, diminishing returns and increasing returns. Factors affecting shifts of the PPF were also considered.

Positive and normative economics were defined. Alternative economic systems were also discussed.

Key points

- Scarcity, referred to as the central problem of economics, implies that there are not enough resources to meet the needs of all economic agents.

- A free good in economics is a good or service for which the opportunity cost of consumption to society is zero.

- An economic good refers to a good or service that is valued by individuals and thus can be sold at a non-negative price in the market.

- In economics we use the term 'opportunity cost' to refer to the cost of one choice in terms of the next best alternative.

- The production possibility frontier (PPF) is a macroeconomic tool that represents the point at which an economy is most efficiently producing its goods and services and, therefore, allocating its resources in the best way possible.

- Positive statements address matters of fact. As such, positive statements are objective statements and made without value judgements, opinions or emotions.

- Normative statements are based on opinion and are not often premised on sound theory.

- An economic system refers to the network of economic agents whose interaction is geared towards answering the fundamental allocation problems of what to produce, how to produce and for whom to produce.

2　The theory of consumer demand

Content

- Utility: total, marginal, cardinal (marginalist approach), ordinal (indifference curve approach)
  - Explanation of diminishing marginal utility
  - The main assumptions and limitations of marginal utility theory
- Indifference curves and the budget constraint (budget lines)
- The law of equi-marginal returns
- The point of tangency of the budget line to the indifference curve
- Income and substitution effects of a price change
- Effective demand
- Deriving the demand curve using the marginal utility as well as the indifference curve approach
- Normal, inferior and Giffen goods using the indifference curve approach
- Shift versus movements along demand curves
- Price and the conditions of demand
- Consumer surplus including graphical representations
- Price, income and cross-elasticities
- Calculation of values of elasticity
- Classification and interpretations (sign and size); including the drawings and interpretations of graphs
- The implications of price elasticity of demand for total spending and revenue
- Factors that determine the price elasticity of demand

Utility and consumer equilibrium

The term 'utility' was first introduced by the British philosopher Jeremy Bentham (1748–1832), but it was not until the publishing of works by Adam Smith (1723–90), David Ricardo (1772–1823), Karl Marx (1818–83) and William Stanley Jevons (1835–82) that the relationship between the value of goods and utility in consumption became clear. Bentham (1789) defined the principle of utility to be:

> property in any object ... to produce pleasure, good or happiness or prevent ... pain evil or unhappiness

An Introduction to the Principles of Morals (1789)

However, it was not until the publishing of the book *Theory of Political Economy* (1871) by Jevons that the relationship between marginal utility, total utility and price entered economic literature.

In the real world, consumers seek to maximise their welfare, subject to the constraints imposed by their income and the market prices of goods and services. Consumers have two principal decision-making tasks when confronting the market:

- which goods to buy
- what quantities of these goods to buy

Example

Utility is individual-specific (subjective). Utility can also vary with the time. For example, in the 'dry season' in Caribbean states (January to May) people may consume more cricket balls and bats, but these same goods are not significantly consumed during the 'wet season' (June to December) because the playing fields are usually soaked.

Example

Jeremy Bentham (1748–1832)

Jeremy Bentham, philosopher and political radical, was the son of a prominent London attorney. Bentham studied law at the highly acclaimed Lincoln's Inn and was accepted by the bar in 1772. Bentham, however, never practised law, but spent most of his time researching and critiquing the existing legal system, advocating strongly for reform.

Bentham is predominantly known for his moral philosophies of utilitarianism. Utilitarianism, as Bentham proposed, is premised on the evaluation of actions based on consequences, in that a person's welfare, for instance, is based on their actions. Bentham strongly advocated for the acceptance of this principle in judicial, social, political and legal affairs. Although Bentham's influence was not widespread while he was alive, his philosophies were carried on by John Stuart Mill and John Austin, both of whom wrote extensively on consumer behaviour in economics.

Thus if a consumer is a vegetarian cricketer, he will obviously not visit the butcher or the frozen meat section of the supermarket. However, if he sees a sports store he may well find himself indulging in some of the goods on offer, as the goods from the sports store will be useful to the cricketer and offer, him satisfaction, while the meat will not.

Goods and services are demanded because they provide satisfaction to consumers. Satisfaction in economics is called utility. Utility is therefore the main substantive determinant of demand. Utility can also be regarded as consumer welfare. Thus it can be said that the consumer will only purchase a commodity if it offers him utility.

Traditionally, the unit of measurement for utility was the util. However, in modern economics, 1 util is equated to $1 and, as such, utility is measured in monetary terms.

The utility that a consumer receives from consuming successive units of a commodity decreases as more of that commodity is consumed. To illustrate this, let us consider the avid cricketer who has lost all his equipment because someone stole it. Assume he now buys a bat and all the other gear except the ball. The cricketer practises with friends who do not have any equipment, so clearly they will need at least one ball. This means that our cricketer will need to get the first ball with some degree of urgency. His welfare from this first ball will therefore be very high. For a second cricket ball, the cricketer will get a lower level of utility as the first one may last for some time. Indeed for every successive ball purchased after the first ball the consumer will receive progressively lower utility, other things constant. This is known as the law of diminishing marginal utility. Marginal utility refers to the extra or additional satisfaction arising from the consumption of an additional unit of a commodity. For example, if the cricketer had to purchase these balls at an auction or through some bargaining process, then he would be willing to pay more for the first ball than for the second ball. For the second ball he would be willing to pay more than for the third ball and so on.

This type of rationale underlies the downward-sloping demand curve, in that, as consumers increase the quantity of a good consumed, their marginal utility falls and so too their willingness to pay. Hence there is an inverse relationship between quantity demanded and price, as discussed later in this chapter. In this regard, therefore, it can be concluded that a consumer's demand for a commodity is based on his marginal rather than total utility function.

Total and marginal utility and the law of diminishing marginal returns

The total utility that a consumer derives from consuming a good is equitable to the total satisfaction the consumer receives. Marginal utility refers to the satisfaction a consumer receives from consuming *an extra unit* of the commodity. Therefore, if the consumer realises a total utility of TU_n from consuming n units of a commodity, and TU_{n-1} from consuming $n-1$ units of the commodity, then we can derive the marginal utility (MU) from consuming the nth unit of a commodity as:

$$MU_{nth} = TU_n - TU_{n-1}$$

In the example from the previous section we noted that as the consumer utilised more cricket balls, the utility he received from each successive ball decreased. This is the law of diminishing marginal utility at work and it may be generalised by stating that:

The law of diminishing marginal utility implies that as increasing amounts of a commodity are consumed, the marginal utility of the additional unit consumed diminishes.

We can sketch the marginal utility curve of a consumer as illustrated in the graph below.

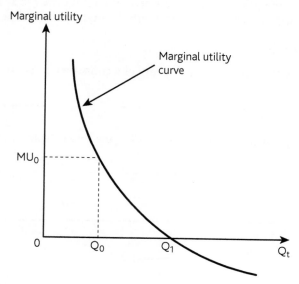

Figure 2.1 *Marginal utility curve*

Observe from Figure 2.1 that after Q_1 units of cricket balls are consumed, the marginal utility of the consumer becomes negative.

To see this, let us consider the extreme case of the cricketer's entire room being filled with cricket balls. Surely if the extra cricket ball has to be placed under his pillow his utility from that ball will be negative, meaning that he will have a higher total utility without it.

The cumulative sum of marginal utilities gives the total utility of the consumer for consuming a commodity.

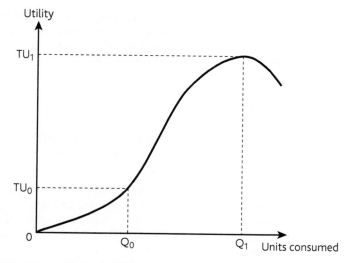

Figure 2.2 *Total utility curve of a consumer*

In Figure 2.2 observe that total utility increases rapidly from 0 to TU_0 in the early stages of consuming the commodity. As more and more of the commodity is consumed, however, observe that the total utility curve increases at a decreasing rate, indicating that marginal utility from each successive unit of the commodity falls. After Q_1 units of the commodity are consumed, the marginal utility of the consumer becomes negative and so the total utility curve turns downward. Marginal utility can therefore be regarded as the slope, or rate of change of the total utility curve, where, when marginal utility equals zero, the total utility is at its highest, and as marginal utility becomes negative, total utility declines.

Numerical example

Table 2.1 shows the total and marginal utility of a consumer consuming cricket balls.

Table 2.1 *Marginal and total utility*

Number of cricket balls	Marginal utility	Total utility
0	0	0
1	45	45
2	40	85
3	39	124
4	37	161
5	34	195
6	30	225
7	25	250
8	19	269
9	12	282
10	4	286

Activity 2.1

Plot the total utility and marginal utility curves using the data in Table 2.1 to the left.

Feedback

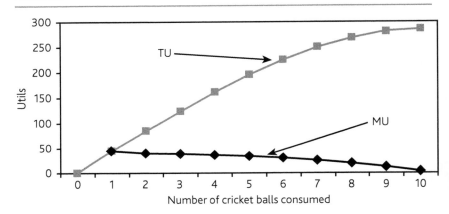

Figure 2.3 *Total utility and marginal utility curves*

Both the table and figure 2.3 indicate that total utility increases first at an increasing, then at a decreasing rate. In addition to which, as long as marginal utility is positive, total utility will increase. Total utility is highest when marginal utility is zero. Total utility declines as marginal utility becomes negative.

Consumer equilibrium

The concepts of total and marginal utility give some insight into the purchasing behaviour of consumers, but it must be considered within the context of consumer income and the market price of goods.

Consider, for example, the situation where for a given commodity the marginal utility derived from the last unit consumed exceeds the market price. In this case the consumer is in disequilibrium, where the satisfaction derived from consuming the last unit is greater than the price they are asked to pay. It would make sense for the consumer to increase their consumption of that commodity. Alternatively, if the marginal utility of the last unit consumed is less than the market price, then the consumer should reduce their consumption.

In a single commodity framework, therefore, the consumer will continue to demand the commodity up to the point where the marginal utility

Example

Theory applications

What is the relationship between the total utility and marginal utility curves?

Consider the relative values of diamonds and water in a situation where the consumer is in a desert.

derived from the last unit consumed is exactly equal to the price the consumer has to pay. The equilibrium purchasing conditions for any single commodity becomes:

$$MUi = Pi$$

or alternatively where:

$$MUi/Pi = 1$$

Derivation of the demand curve

Using the single commodity situation, the principle of consumer equilibrium can be used to map out the relationship between changes in a commodity's own price and changes in quantity demanded by the consumer. As discussed above, the consumer will continue to demand the commodity up to the point where marginal utility of the last unit consumed is equal to price. As the market price falls, consumers will therefore increase consumption of the commodity in order to restore equilibrium. Table 2.2 shows the trends in burgers consumed per week given marginal utility and price.

If the market price per burger is $16, then the consumer will consume burgers up to the point where their marginal utility equals 16 or rather up to the point where the ratio of marginal utility to price is 1. Using the information in Table 2.2 below, it can be concluded that the consumer will purchase two burgers per week given a market price of $16. If the market price falls to $12 per burger, then the consumer will be in disequilibrium given that 16/12 =1.33. To restore equilibrium the consumer will increase their consumption up to the point where the marginal utility of the last burger consumed is equal to the market price of $12. As a consequence, the consumer increases their consumption of burgers to three per week.

Assuming now that the price per burger falls to $9, the consumer is again in disequilibrium given that the ratio of marginal utility to market price is greater than 1 (1.33). To restore equilibrium the consumer increases their consumption of burgers to four per week. Table 2.2 below also illustrates the equilibrium conditions if the market price falls to $7 and $6 respectively. Note that as the price falls the consumer increases their consumption of burgers in order to restore equilibrium. This information can be summarised in Table 2.3 below, which plots the various pairs of equilibrium price and quantity demanded of burgers. Note that the price is equal to the marginal utility of consumption.

Table 2.2 *Marginal utility of burgers consumed per week*

Qty	MU	MU/P, when P = 16	MU/P, when P = 12	MU/P, when P = 9	MU/P, when P = 7	MU/P, when P = 6
1	21	1.31	1.75	2.33	3.00	3.50
2	16	1.00	1.33	1.78	2.29	2.67
3	12	0.75	1.00	1.33	1.71	2.00
4	9	0.56	0.75	1.00	1.29	1.50
5	7	0.44	0.58	0.78	1.00	1.17
6	6	0.38	0.50	0.67	0.86	1.00

Table 2.3 *The demand schedule*

Qty	Price
2	16
3	12
4	9
5	7
6	6

Plotting this data gives the downward-sloping demand curve for burgers per week.

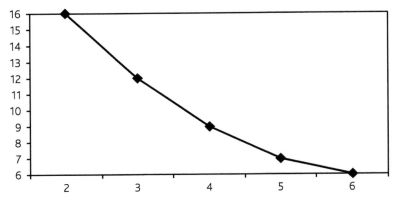

Figure 2.4 *Demand curve for burgers per week*

Consumer equilibrium: the equimarginal principle

In a multi-good framework the same principle can apply. That is, the consumer aims to equalise the ratio of marginal utility to price for every good consumed. For simplicity assume that a consumer's basket of goods consists of only two commodities, a and b. So that:

$$MUa/Pa = 1 = MUb/Pb$$

$$MUa/Pa = MUb/Pb$$

$$MUa/MUb = Pa/Pb$$

This is the principle of *equimarginal utility*. It illustrates consumer equilibrium in a situation where the basket of goods consumed consists of more than one commodity, with varying market price levels.

Considering the example above, where it is assumed that the price of good a falls, the consumer is no longer in equilibrium. To restore equilibrium the consumer would purchase more of good a, as its relative price has fallen as compared to good b. As the consumer substitutes more of good a for good b the marginal utility of good a falls while the marginal utility of good b increases. These marginal utilities would adjust until once again the condition of *equimarginal utility*, or *consumer equilibrium*, is re-attained.

Limitations of the cardinalist approach

One of the key limitations of the cardinalist approach was highlighted by Pareto. He alluded to the fact that individuals were better able to rank their preferences rather than to assign a specific value to them. For example, he highlighted that an individual can prefer bundle A over bundle B, rather than assign a utility value of 20 to A as compared to 15 to B.

Another limitation of this theory relates to the fact that satisfaction cannot be measured objectively, in that the satisfaction assigned to the consumption of an ice cream cone by individual A, for example, is not the same as that assigned by individual B. Furthermore, the satisfaction assigned to the consumption of a particular good may vary over time.

This theory is also flawed because it measures utility in monetary terms. Money in itself does not have a constant marginal utility. In fact, as income increases, the marginal utility of money falls. As such, money cannot be used as an objective measuring rod for utility.

In light of these limitations new theories of consumer behaviour have been proposed. One such theory is the theory of indifference curve analysis.

Indifference curve analysis is a tool used in economics to explain consumer behaviour in different market situations. Indifference curve analysis has two components: the indifference curve and the budget line.

Activity 2.2

1 The table below shows the utility that Alex gets from the consumption of DVD movies and comic books. Alex has $100 per month to spend on DVD movies and comic books. DVD movies cost $20 each and comic books cost $20 each.

Quantity	Utility from DVD movies	Utility from comic books
0	0	0
1	30	30
2	40	38
3	48	44
4	54	46
5	58	47

   a Define the term 'marginal utility'.
   b Calculate Alex's marginal utility for:
      i   DVD movies
      ii comic books.
   c Calculate the marginal utility per dollar of Alex's consumption choices.
2 State the optimatal number of DVD movies and comic books that Alex will consume in one month.

Feedback

1 a Marginal utility is defined as the change in total utility that occurs when an additional unit of a good or service is consumed.
   b and c

Quantity	Utility from DVD movies	Utility from comic books	Marginal utility of DVD movies	Marginal utility of comic books	Marginal utility per $ of DVD movies	Marginal utility per $ of comic books
0	0	0	0	0		
1	30	30	30	30	1.50	1.50
2	40	38	10	8	0.50	0.40
3	48	44	8	6	0.40	0.30
4	54	46	6	2	0.30	0.10
5	58	47	4	1	0.20	0.05

2 This is the value that meets the equilibrium marginal utility condition while at the same time making use of all of the $100 income. Alex will therefore consume three DVD movies and two comic books in a month.

Indifference curve analysis

An indifference curve is the locus of all the possible combinations of two or more goods, or group of goods or services, which yield the same level of satisfaction to the consumer. For illustrative purposes, consider the data in Table 2.4 below which shows the combinations of clothing and food that yield the same level of satisfaction to a consumer.

Table 2.4 *Alternative bundles conferring equal satisfaction*

Bundle	Clothing	Food
A	30	1
B	18	2
C	13	3
D	10	4
E	8	5
F	7	6

We use this information to plot the indifference curve (IC) for the consumer as shown in figure 2.5.

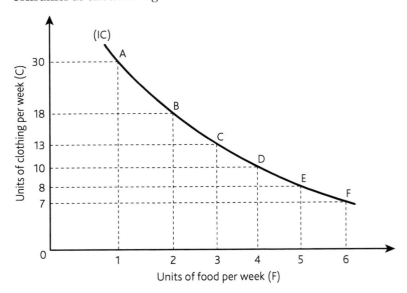

Figure 2.5 *Indifference curve*

In the real world, economic agents make trade-offs between the goods they consume; indifference curve analysis can help to make these trade-offs clearer. In the indifference curve above, it can be shown that in moving from market bundle A to B the consumer gives up 12 units of A to obtain a single unit of B. Similarly, to move from market bundle B to C the consumer gives up five units of clothing for a single unit of food. The slope of the indifference curve illustrates that the consumer will be willing to give up less and less units of clothing for food if they wish to remain at the same level of satisfaction, that is, on the same indifference curve. To quantify the amount of clothing a consumer is willing to give up for food, economists will calculate the marginal rate of substitution (MRS). The marginal rate of substitution of food for clothes is therefore the slope of the indifference curve. From the Figure 2.5 above, it is clear that the slope of the indifference curve falls continually.

Properties of indifference curves

■ Indifference curves do not intersect. This is a mathematical impossibility in that it would imply that one point is characterised by two levels of satisfaction.

■ Indifference curves slope downwards from left to right. This shows that there is an opportunity cost involved in increasing the consumption of one commodity as against the other. The slope is also called the marginal rate of substitution.

■ The curve is convex to the origin. The convexity of the curve reflects the nature of the opportunity cost, that is, it is decreasing over the length of the curve.

■ The further away the indifference curve is from the origin, the higher the level of satisfaction.

■ There are an infinite number of indifference curves in welfare space; collectively these are called an indifference map.

Indifference map

An indifference map represents a set of indifference curves that illustrate the preferences of a consumer. In figure 2.6 below, I_5 represents the highest level of welfare and I_1 the lowest. Observe that:

$$I_5 > I_4 > I_3 > I_2 > I_1$$

where '>' implies preferred.

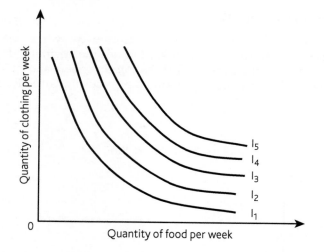

Figure 2.6 *Indifference map*

Budget line

The budget line of a consumer shows all the combinations of clothing (C) and food (F) that a consumer can buy given the prices of clothing (P_c) and food (P_f) and the consumer's money income (Y).

Algebraically:

$$Y = P_c C + P_f F$$

where C is the number of units of clothing purchased at the price P_c and F is the number of units of food purchased at the price P_f. The right-hand side of the equation above reads that the sum of expenses on clothing ($P_c C$) and food ($P_f F$) is equal to the income of the household, assuming that the consumer does not save any proportion of their income.

With this budget line, the intercept on the vertical (clothing) axis is Y/P_c and the intercept on the horizontal (food) axis is Y/P_f. The slope of the budget line therefore, is $-P_f/P_c$. We can plot this budget line as illustrated in the diagram below.

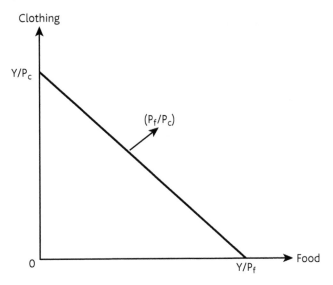

Figure 2.7 *Budget line*

Changes in income (Y)

The budget line of a consumer will shift outwards away from the origin if Y increases, *ceteris paribus* and inward towards the origin if Y decreases. Thus let the original income level of the consumer be Y and let Y_1 and Y_2 be income levels lower and higher than Y respectively. Given P_c, then:

$$Y_1/P_c < Y/P_c < Y_2/P_c$$

and

$$Y_1/P_f < Y/P_f < Y_2/P_f$$

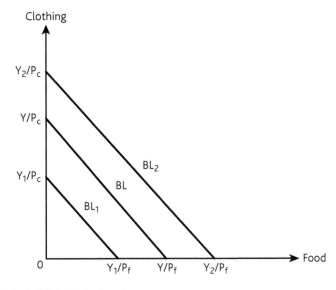

Figure 2.8 *A shift in the budget line*

Other things constant, an increase in income allows the household to buy more of both goods (Y_2/P_f and Y_2/P_c) while a decrease in income means that the household has to buy less of both goods (Y_1/P_f and Y_1/P_c).

Feedback

Income = 10, P_f = 2, P_c = 1

Q_f	Q_c
5	0
4	2
3	4
2	6
1	8
0	10

Income = 20, P_f = 2, P_c = 1

Q_f	Q_c
10	0
8	4
6	8
4	12
2	16
0	20

> **Activity 2.3**
>
> Plot the budget lines when income is assumed to be $10 and also when income increases to $20. Assume also that the price of food is $2 per unit and $1 per unit for clothes.

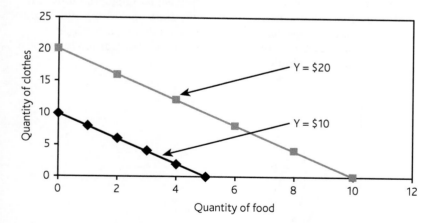

Figure 2.9 *The budget line changes when income changes*

Price changes and the budget line

If the price of one of the goods entering a consumer's market bundle changes, then the slope of the consumer's budget line will change. For illustrative purposes, let us consider what happens to the budget line when the price of food changes. Specifically, let P_f be the original price of food and let P^1_f and P^2_f represent lower and higher prices of food respectively. Clearly,

$$Y/P^1_f < Y/P_f < Y_2/P^2_f$$

These changes can be illustrated as shown in Figure 2.10.

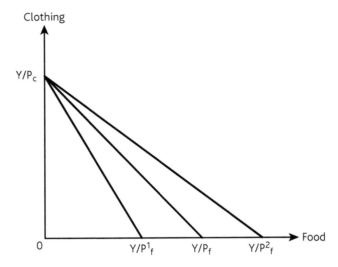

Figure 2.10 *The budget line when the price of food changes*

Consumer equilibrium

The consumer is in equilibrium when they maximise the welfare they can obtain subject to the constraints of their income and the market prices of the commodities they purchase. Graphically, consumer equilibrium occurs where the consumer's budget line is just tangential to the highest attainable indifference curve. In Figure 2.11 this occurs at point B where the consumer's budget line is just tangential to IC_2. In equilibrium this consumer will purchase C_2 units of clothing and F_2 units of food. Note that in equilibrium the marginal rate of substitution of clothes for food is equal to the price ratio of these two commodities, or to the slope of the budget line.

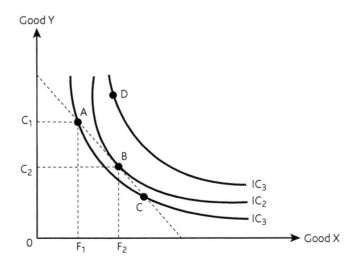

Figure 2.11 *Consumer equilibrium using indifference curve analysis*

Algebraically,

$$MRS_{f,c} = P_f/P_c$$

Point D is not attainable given the consumer's income and the prices of food and clothing currently existing on the marketplace, while points A and C are obtainable but are not welfare maximising points.

The price consumption curve and the demand curve

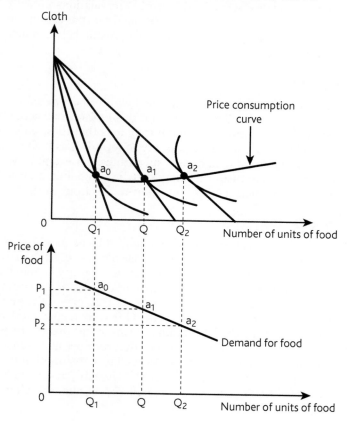

Figure 2.12 *Derivation of the demand curve for a normal good*

In Figure 2.12 the upper panel shows the varying slopes of the budget line of a consumer at the alternative price levels for food P^1_f, P_f and P^2_f where, $P^2_f < P_f < P1_f$. With these alternative price levels for food, the consumer in their various equilibrium conditions purchases Q_1 units of food at the price P^1_f, Q units at the price P_f and Q_2 units at the price P^2_f. The second panel of this same figure plots the price of food on the vertical axis against the respective quantities of food demanded on the horizontal axis. Thus at price P^1_f, Q_1 units of food is purchased while at price P_f, Q units are purchased and so on. The points a_0, a_1 and a_2 when combined in the lower panel of the figure trace the demand curve for food by this consumer. Note that the points a_0, a_1 and a_2 in the upper part of the figure trace out the consumer's price consumption curve.

The income and substitution effect of a price change: the Hicksian approach

Normal goods

Normal goods in economics are so defined by their relationship with price and consumer income. There is an inverse relationship between quantity demanded and the price, in that as price increases quantity demanded falls and vice versa. With regard to its relationship with income, as consumer income increases demand for that commodity also increases. In this regard, there is a direct relationship between demand and consumer income.

Inferior goods

An inferior good differs from a normal good with respect to its relationship with income. The demand for this type of good actually falls when income rises. An important point to note is that these goods are not intrinsically inferior in quality, but are so regarded, as higher income earners may switch to more luxurious substitutes. For example, when a consumers' income increases they may switch from public transport to their own vehicle as their mode of transport to and from work.

Giffen goods

A Giffen good is a special type of inferior good. The demand for such goods is directly related to its price, such that increases in the market price of the commodity results in an increase in quantity demanded and a decrease in quantity demanded when the market price of the commodity falls. There are few examples of such goods. In fact, one of the first commodities that was identified as having Giffen good characteristics was the Irish potato. During the Irish famine it was found that as the price of potatoes increased, people were so poor that they began to substitute other staples and meat with potatoes. As such its consumption increased. Another example was empirically observed by Robert Jensen and Nolan Miller, who noted that as the price of rice increased, the poor Chinese communities actually bought more rice.

Normal goods

The incomes and substitution effects of a price change can be decomposed using the Hicksian framework. The substitution effect is defined as the change in the combination of goods purchased due to a change in the relative prices. The income effect refers to a change in the combinations of goods due to a change in the level of real income, where real income is defined as the purchasing power of money. More generally, the substitution effect says that, on average, when the price of a commodity increases, consumers will tend to substitute other cheaper commodities for the relatively more expensive ones. Also, when the prices of commodities increase, assuming that consumers' money income is fixed, consumers' real income falls, that is, their capacity to purchase all goods.

The substitution effect of a price change is always negative, that is, as price falls quantity demanded increases, while the income effect may be negative or positive. For a normal good the income effect is positive, that is, as income increases the demand for the commodity increases. A negative income effect implies that as income increases demand falls.

In Figure 2.13, consumer equilibrium occurs at the point where the budget line, BL_0, is tangential to the indifference curve, IC_0. Assuming

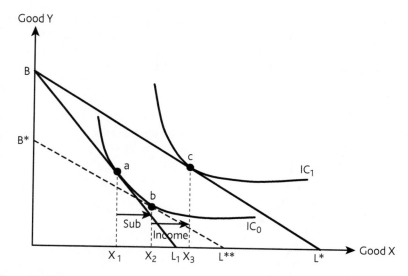

Figure 2.13 *Decomposition of the income and substitution effects for a normal good*

then that the price of commodity X falls, the budget line will pivot outward to the right to BL*, where the new consumer equilibrium occurs on a higher indifference curve IC_1.

For the purposes of analysis, let us assume that the good X is normal. The total increase in consumption of good X, from X_1 to X_3, is called the total effect. To decompose the total effect into the income and the substitution effects it is necessary to introduce into the analysis a hypothetical budget line, B* L**. The adjustment in income that this represents is referred to as the compensating variation. This is parallel to the new budget line BL* but tangential to the original indifference curve. Including this point of tangency in the analysis, the pure substitution effect is given as the difference between those two combinations that occur at different price relatives, that is b–a, while the income effect is shown by the difference in combinations on two different real income levels, that is, points c–b. The total price effect therefore is c–a.

For a normal good, the negative substitution effect is reinforced by a positive income effect, making the total effect negative. So as price falls, quantity demanded increases, *ceteris paribus*, that is, from X_1 to X_3.

Inferior goods

Initial conditions are such that the consumer is in equilibrium where the initial budget line BL_1 is tangential to IC_1. In Figure 2.14 on page 36, it is assumed that the good X is inferior, and that the price of X falls. The budget line pivots to BL_2, where the consumer is at a new equilibrium level, on a higher indifference curve IC_2. The total change in consumption from X_1 to X_2 is called the total effect. As above, the income and substitution effects can be decomposed by introducing into the analysis B*L*, which is parallel to the new budget line and tangential to the original budget line. The substitution effect is shown as a, while the income effect is b.

When the price of good X falls, the substitution effect is negative. This implies that the fall in the price of the good leads to an increase in the quantity demanded of the good. The income effect for inferior goods, however, is negative. This means that an increase in real income leads to a fall in the demand for good X. In Figure 2.14 on page 36 the substitution effect occurs from X_1 to X_2, while the negative income effect occurs from X_2 to X_3, so that the overall price effect, X_1 to X_3, is still negative, implying that for inferior goods the effect of a fall in price is an increase in the quantity of the good consumed.

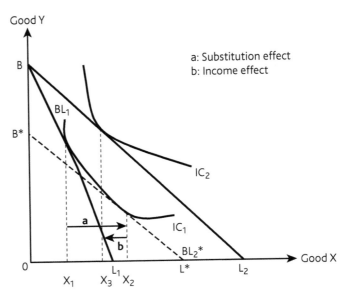

Figure 2.14 *Income and substitution effects for an inferior good*

Giffen goods

Giffen goods are an extreme type of inferior goods. For the Giffen good, the negative income effect more than offsets the negative substitution effect. In Figure 2.15, for a reduction in the price of X, the Giffen good results in a situation where less of the commodity is demanded by the consumer.

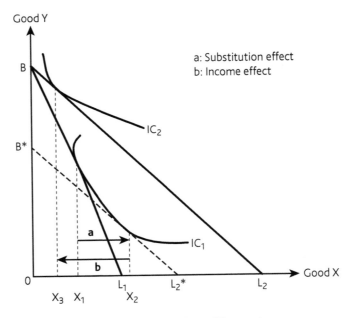

Figure 2.15 *Income and substitution effects for a Giffen good*

Distinguishing between income and substitution effects of a price change: the Slutsky approach

The Slutsky approach analyses the income and substitution effect differently from that of the Hicksian methodology. In Figure 2.16, considering that the price of a normal good X falls, consumer equilibrium moves from point a to b. This increase in consumption of good X is called the price effect, which can be decomposed into the substitution and income effects.

To isolate the substitution effect, the Slutsky approach imposes a hypothetical budget line, B*L* through the original equilibrium point, a, which is parallel to the new budget line. This hypothetical budget line is tangential to a new indifference curve IC_1^1, giving a new consumer equilibrium point b. The income and substitution effects can now be decomposed. The shifts in consumer equilibrium from points a to b is known as the substitution while the shift from b to c is the income effect.

Example
Evgeny Evgenievich Slutsky (1880–1946)

This Russian genius mastered the disciplines of mathematics and the physical sciences. Although his first degree was in engineering, his passion for politics enticed him to pursue another degree in Political Economics. In 1911 he graduated with the Gold Medal for his paper on 'The theory of marginal utility'. His work in the area of economics continued and in 1912 he published his first text, *The Theory of Correlation*. 1920 he became a professor at the Kiev Institute of Commerce.

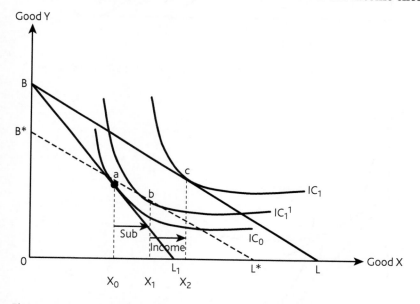

Figure 2.16 *Decomposition of the income and substitution effects for a normal good*

In Figure 2.17 on page 38, considering that the price of an inferior good X falls, consumer equilibrium moves from point a to c. To isolate the substitution effect, the Slutsky approach imposes a hypothetical budget line, B*L*, through the original equilibrium point, a, which is parallel to the new budget line. This hypothetical budget line is tangential to a new indifference curve IC_1^1, giving a new consumer equilibrium point b. The income and substitution effects can now be decomposed. The shifts in consumer equilibrium from points a to b is known as the substitution while the shift from b to c is the income effect.

In Figure 2.18 on page 38, considering that the price of a Giffen good X falls, consumer equilibrium moves from point a to c. The Slutsky approach imposes a hypothetical budget line, B*L*, through the original equilibrium point, a, which is parallel to the new budget line. This hypothetical budget line is tangential to a new indifference curve IC_1^1, giving a new consumer equilibrium point b. The income and substitution effects can now be decomposed. The shifts in consumer equilibrium from points a to b is known as the substitution while the shift from b to c is the income effect.

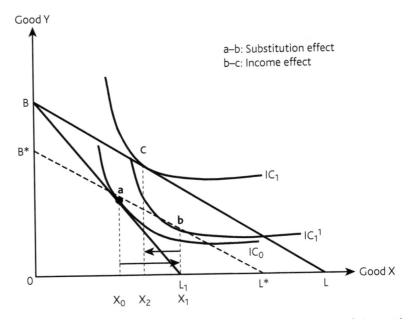

Figure 2.17 *Decomposition of the income and substitution effects for an inferior good*

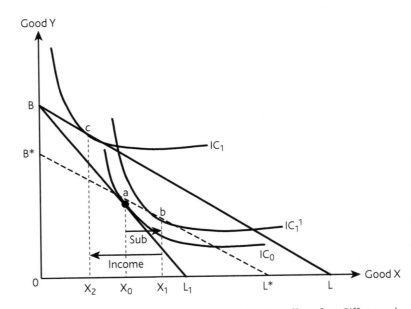

Figure 2.18 *Decomposition of the income and substitution effects for a Giffen good*

The theory of demand: effective demand

There are two types of demand in economics, desired demand and effective demand. Desired demand is an expressed preference for having a particular good or service. Effective demand is desired demand that is 'backed' by the capability to acquire the good or service, that is, effective demand refers to the willingness and the ability to pay for the commodity.

Desired demand cannot be measured because of the unlimited nature of wants. Effective demand, however, can be measured and, as such, demand in economics is effective rather than desired demand.

Specifying the demand function

The quantity demanded of any commodity n (Q^d_n) is given by the following functional notation:

$$Q^d_n = D\,[P_n,\ P1\ \dots\ P_{n-1},\ Adv,\ Y,\ E,\ W,\ \lambda,\ exp^n]$$

D: a taste parameter that shapes the entire demand curve

P_n: the price of the commodity n

$P_1\ \dots\ P_{n-1}$: the price of all other commodities on the market

Adv: advertising

Y: the income of the household in question

E: a host of sociological factors

W: wealth of the consumer

exp^n: expectations

λ: exogenous random elements, for example war, famine, etc.

The process by which we use economic theory to determine the factors that influence the demand for a commodity is called specifying the demand function.

The demand schedule

The demand schedule is a tabular representation of the relationship between the price of a commodity and the quantity of it demanded.

Let us consider the demand for ackee by a Jamaican housewife. The schedule in Table 2.5 shows the quantity of ackee demanded at various prices per dozen.

The information on the schedule above can be represented using a graph, in which case the graph is called the demand curve. The demand curve of the housewife for ackee is shown in Figure 2.19.

Note that the demand curve is downward sloping, which is indicative of the negative relationship between price and quantity demanded. This relationship holds true for all normal and inferior goods.

Table 2.5 *Demand schedule*

Price of a dozen ackee	Dozens of ackee demanded
1	120
2	100
3	80
4	60
5	40
6	20

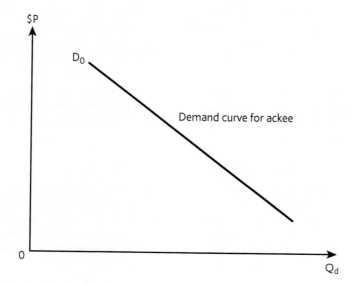

Figure 2.19 *Demand curve*

Difference between a change in demand and a change in the quantity demanded

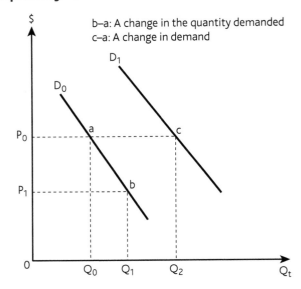

Figure 2.20 *The difference between a change in demand and a change in the quantity demanded*

Figure 2.20 illustrates the difference between a change in demand and a change in quantity demanded. Consider the demand curve D_0. At the price $\$P_0$ the consumer will demand Q_0 units of ackee while at the price $\$P_1$ the consumer will demand Q_1 units of ackee. The movement from Q_0 to Q_1 represents a change in the quantity demand of ackee. The movement from Q_1 to Q_2 occurs because of an increase in demand for ackee. Note that the quantities Q_0 and Q_2 are both demanded at the same price level P_0, indicating that the conditions under which demand is made has changed.

A change in the quantity demanded of a commodity is represented by a movement along the demand curve, while a change in demand is represented by a shift of the demand curve.

A movement along the curve can either be a contraction or an expansion of quantity demanded and is caused by a change in the price of the commodity. A reduction in price results in an expansion of quantity demanded, while an increase in price results in a contraction of quantity demanded.

A shift, however, is caused by a change in any of the factors that affect demand other than the commodity's own price. A rightward shift is indicative of an increase in demand while a leftward shift is indicative of a fall in demand.

Market demand function

The market demand curve represents the sum of the individual consumers in an economy. In Table 2.6 we show the demand for ackee by consumers in Jamaica. For simplicity, we assume there are only two consumers, but this does not affect the generalisation to many more consumers. The market demand represents the sum of the demands of consumer 1 and consumer 2.

Table 2.6 *Market demand schedule for ackee in a particular week*

Price ackee	Q^1_{dc}	Q^2_{dc}	Market demand = $Q^1_{dc} + Q^2_{dc}$
1	9	12	21
2	8	11	19
3	7	10	17
4	6	9	15
5	5	8	13
6	4	7	11
7	3	6	9
8	2	5	7
9	1	4	5
10	0	3	3

The market demand curve as illustrated in Figure 2.21 is downward sloping. It reflects how much of a commodity will be demanded by all the consumers in an economy given their preference structures and the price levels in the marketplace.

The market demand schedule is analogous to the individual consumer's demand schedule and shows how the entire quantity of a commodity that the market demands changes when the price of the commodity changes.

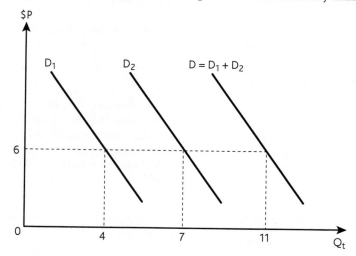

Figure 2.21 *Individual and market demand curves*

Consumer surplus

Consumer surplus refers to the benefit obtained by consumers by purchasing a commodity at a particular market price. Consumer surplus occurs where there is a difference between how the consumers value a commodity as opposed to how the market values the commodity. *It is the difference in price between what the consumer was willing to pay and what the consumer actually pays to obtain the commodity.*

For example, Sarah places a personal value on apples equal to $10.00, while the market price or market value of the commodity is $5.00. The consumer surplus derived on purchase of the apples is the difference in individual vs market valuation of the commodity, $5.00.

The concept of consumer surplus can be shown graphically on a demand curve, as the area below the demand curve, above the price line and to the right of the price axis. This is shown in the Figure 2.22 below as the area ABP_0.

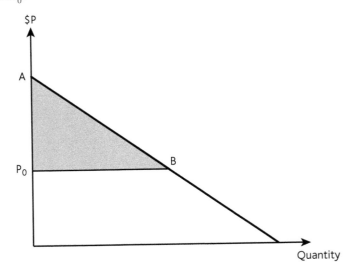

Figure 2.22 *Consumer surplus*

Elasticity

Elasticity is the measure of the responsiveness of the change in one variable to changes in another.

Elasticity of demand

Elasticity of demand therefore measures the degree of responsiveness of demand to changes in the factors that affect demand. In economics, we focus on three variables in terms of analysing how these affect demand. These variables are price (in which case the measure is called price elasticity of demand), income (income elasticity of demand) and the price of other goods (cross-elasticity of demand).

Price elasticity of demand

Price point elasticity of demand

Price elasticity of demand is a measure of the responsiveness of the quantity demanded of a commodity n to changes in the price of that commodity, other things constant.

Algebraically,

$$PED = \frac{\Delta P_n}{\Delta Q_n^d}$$

where

% ΔQ_n^d: percentage change in the quantity demanded of commodity n

% ΔP_n: percentage change in the price of the commodity n

The demand curve is downward sloping, which reflects a negative relationship between price and quantity demanded. This means that an increase (decrease) in price will lead to a decrease (increase) in the quantity demanded. To correct for this, economists insert a 'negative' sign in front of the formula above so that all the PED values become positive: $PED = (-) \% \Delta Q^d_n / \% \Delta P_n$

Price elasticity of demand adopts a value within the theoretical range:

$$0 < |PED| < \infty$$

when

$PED = 0$, this indicates perfect price inelasticity

$0 < |PED| < 1$, price inelasticity

$|PED| = 1$, unit elasticity

$1 < |PED| < \infty$, price elasticity

$|PED| = \infty$, perfectly price elastic.

Diagrammatically, we can represent perfect price elasticity and perfect price inelasticity as shown in the diagrams below.

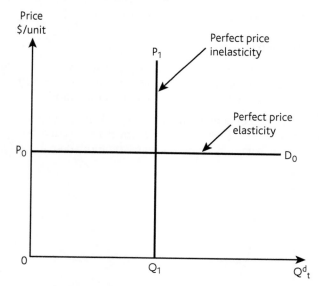

Figure 2.23 *Ranges of price elasticity*

Perfect price inelasticity indicates that changes in price have no effect on the quantity demanded of the commodity. Examples of these goods may be life-saving drugs where the consumer may have no choice but to purchase the good. A perfectly elastic demand curve, however, indicates that consumers are only willing to purchase the commodity at a particular price level and at no other. Any changes in price will result in quantity demanded falling to zero.

Figure 2.24 on page 44 shows that along a linear demand curve the price elasticity of demand fluctuates from perfectly elastic (PED = ∞) to perfectly inelastic (PED = 0). At the midpoint of the demand curve, the PED = 1 indicates that a change in price leads to an exact proportionate change in quantity demanded.

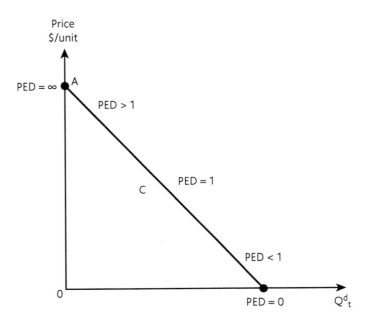

Figure 2.24 *Ranges of elasticity on the demand curve*

Arc price elasticity

The formula outlined above is for elasticity at any point on the demand curve. Because the elasticity value changes at every point on the demand curve, economists calculate arc price elasticity of demand.

The arc price elasticity of demand is utilised to calculate the price elasticity of demand between two price levels. Consider the demand curve below, which shows two prices P_1 and P_2 and the associated quantity demanded Q_1 and Q_2.

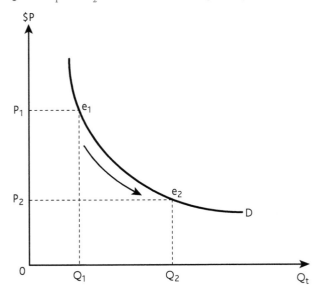

Figure: 2.25 *Arc elasticity of demand*

The two price levels considered here are P_1 and P_2 with the direction of the change in price occurring from P_1 to P_2. To calculate the arc price elasticity of demand we use:

$$PED = \dfrac{\dfrac{Q_2 - Q_1}{\left(\dfrac{Q_2 + Q_1}{2}\right)}}{\dfrac{P_2 - P_1}{\left(\dfrac{P_2 + P_1}{2}\right)}} = -\dfrac{Q_2 - Q_1}{P_2 - P_1} \cdot \dfrac{P_2 + P_1}{Q_2 + Q_1}$$

where

$\dfrac{Q_2 + Q_1}{2}$ represents the average quantity demanded when the price

changes from P_1 to P_2, and $\dfrac{P_2 + P_1}{2}$, the average price level.

Example

Theory application

Consider the following formula for elasticity of demand.

$$\dfrac{Q_2 - Q_1}{Q_1} \div \dfrac{P_2 - P_1}{P_1}$$

This formula can give different values of PED between two points. For example, consider the following demand schedule.

P$	QTY
7	900
6	1,900

The PED when prices increase from $6 to $7 can be evaluated as follows:

$$\dfrac{(900 - 1,900)}{1,900} \times \dfrac{6}{(7 - 6)} = 3.16$$

The PED when price decreases from $7 to $6 can be evaluated as follows:

$$\dfrac{(1,900 - 900)}{900} \times \dfrac{7}{(6 - 7)} = 7.78$$

To avoid getting two different values we use the average of the quantities and the average of the two prices (mid-point formula) as follows:

$$PED = \dfrac{\dfrac{Q_2 - Q_1}{\left(\dfrac{Q_2 + Q_1}{2}\right)}}{\dfrac{P_2 - P_1}{\left(\dfrac{P_2 + P_1}{2}\right)}} = -\dfrac{Q_2 - Q_1}{P_2 - P_1} \cdot \dfrac{P_2 + P_1}{Q_2 + Q_1}$$

The PED for the above example, assuming that prices increased from $6 to $7, can therefore be evaluated as follows:

$$PED = \dfrac{\dfrac{900 - 1,900}{\left(\dfrac{900 + 1,900}{2}\right)}}{\dfrac{7 - 6}{\left(\dfrac{7 + 6}{2}\right)}} = -\dfrac{900 - 1,900}{7 - 6} \cdot \dfrac{7 + 6}{900 + 1,900} = 4.64$$

Activity 2.4

Calculate the arc elasticity of demand between each consecutive point on the demand curve below.

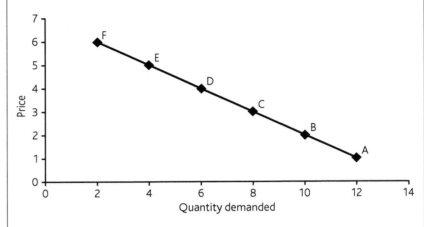

Figure 2.26 *Demand curve*

Feedback

Price	Q^d	Labels		Arc elasticity values
1	120	A		
2	100	B	A to B	−0.03
3	80	C	B to C	−0.05
4	60	D	C to D	−0.08
5	40	E	D to E	−0.16
6	20	F	E to F	−0.44

Factors influencing price elasticity of demand

- Substitutes: the greater the number of substitutes for a commodity, the greater the price elasticity of demand.
- Share of income: the greater the share of a consumer's income that a commodity absorbs, the greater the price elasticity of demand for that commodity. Thus a car will have a greater price elasticity of demand than table salt.
- Type of goods; necessary and luxury goods: some goods are staples while others are luxuries. A staple good forms an integral part of the diet. For CARICOM nationals, staple goods include rice, yam, cassava and flour, while luxury goods include expensive watches, expensive sports cars, and so on. In general, necessary/staple goods have a lower price elasticity of demand than luxury goods.
- Width of definition of the commodity: the narrower the definition of the commodity the higher the PED. Thus food will have an overall lower level of PED than say peanuts or cabbage.
- Time: in the short run, consumers have fairly constant tastes. The taste of a consumer, however, takes time to evolve. Over time, therefore, the PED is greater than in the short run as people's taste can change in response to price changes.

The implications of price elasticity for total spending

Revenue is equal to the price × quantity sold. The amount of revenue earned is directly related to the elasticity of demand. Price elasticity of demand refers to the coefficient that shows the degree of response of quantity demanded to changes in price. This degree of change in quantity demanded and price has implications for the level of total revenue earned.

When demand is price elastic, a given change in price results in a more than proportional change in quantity demanded, while if demand is inelastic there is a less than proportional change in quantity demanded. When demand is unitary, a given price change results in a proportional change in quantity demanded.

Table 2.7 gives the summary of how revenue is affected by price changes over the various ranges of elasticity.

Table 2.7 *Elasticity, price changes and revenue response*

Elasticity	Price change	Revenue response
Elastic	Increase (decrease)	Decrease (increase)
Unitary	Increase (decrease)	Constant (constant)
Inelastic	Increase (decrease)	Increase (decrease)

Income elasticity of demand

Income elasticity of demand may be defined as a measure of the degree of responsiveness of the quantity demanded of a commodity n on account of a change in the income of the household.

$$YED = \%\ \Delta\ Q^d / \%\ \Delta\ in\ Y$$

Theoretically income elasticity can carry any value in the range $\infty < YED < \infty$. This theoretical range can be further subdivided as follows:

- $YED < 0$: negative income elasticity (inferior goods). For these goods an increase in income leads to a decrease in the quantity of the good consumed.
- $YED = 0$: zero income elasticity. For these goods an increase in income has no effect on the quantity of the good consumed.
- $0 < YED < 1$: income inelasticity. For income inelastic goods, an increase in income leads to a less than proportionate change in the quantity of the good consumed. Necessity goods often have a YED that is less than 1.
- $YED = 1$: unit income elasticity.
- $1 < YED < \infty$: income elasticity. For these goods an increase in income has a more than proportionate effect on the quantity of the good consumed by the household. Luxuries often have a YED that is in excess of 1.

The income elasticity of demand for a commodity can fluctuate over time as the income of a household changes. Let us consider the demand for potatoes as shown in figure 2.27 on page 48. When the household's income is low, every increase in household income is matched by an increase in the demand for potatoes. As the income of the household increases and the household can afford to buy more staples, such as flour and yam, so the demand for potatoes tapers off during the income range Y_0 to Y_1. After the income level Y_1, however, the household may actually reduce its demand for potatoes and purchase packaged mashed potatoes with cheese or garlic sauce.

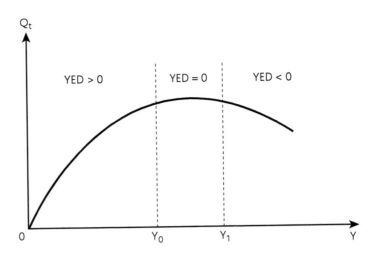

Figure 2.27 *Ranges of income elasticity of demand*

Activity 2.5

Look at the changes in consumer income and demand over time to determine the YED for the commodity X.

$Y	Q_x per month
4,000	2.5
6,000	5.0
8,000	7.5
10,000	9.0
12,000	10.0
14,000	9.5
16,000	9.0

Feedback

$Y	Q_x per month	% ΔQ_x	% ΔY	YED	Interpretation
4,000	2.5				
6,000	5.0	100.00	50.00	2.00	Demand is income elastic over this range and is defined as a normal good with some luxury attribute
8,000	7.5	50.00	33.33	1.50	Demand is income elastic over this range and is defined as a normal good with some luxury attribute
10,000	9.0	20.00	25.00	0.80	Demand is income inelastic over this range and is defined as a normal good that has some type of staple attribute
12,000	10.0	11.11	20.00	0.56	Demand is income inelastic over this range and is defined as a normal good that has some type of staple attribute
14,000	9.5	−5.00	16.67	−0.30	Demand is income inelastic over this range and is defined as inferior
16,000	9.0	−5.26	14.29	−0.37	Demand is income inelastic over this range and is defined as inferior

---

Cross-price elasticity of demand

Cross-elasticity of demand may be defined as a measure of the degree of responsiveness of the demand for a commodity X due to changes in the price of another commodity Y. Cross-elasticity of demand (CED) is calculated as:

$$CED_{X,Y} = \frac{\% \, \Delta \, Q^d_X}{\% \, \Delta \, P_Y}$$

The theoretical range of the cross-elasticity of demand is:

$-\infty < CED < \infty$ where

$-\infty < CED < 0$ complementary goods, is, the CED value is negative

$0 < CED < \infty$ substitutable goods, that is, the CED value is positive

Complementary goods are goods that are jointly demanded because they are used together. Some examples are camera and film or bread and cheese.

Substitutes on the other hand are goods that can be used in place of each other because they satisfy the same need to the consumer. An example of substitutable goods might be Coca-Cola and Pepsi.

Activity 2.6

The original price of the commodity Y is $8 and the quantity demanded for the commodity X stands at 80 units. Calculate the CED if the price of Y changes to $12, with the demand for X increasing to 100 units. What is the relationship between these two commodities X and Y?

Feedback

CED = (20/80)/(4/8)

    = (1/4)/(1/2)

    = 2/4

    = ½

Conclusion: the two goods X and Y are substitutes.

Activity 2.7

The original price of the commodity Y is $20, with the quantity demanded for the commodity X being 80 units. Calculate and interpret the value of CED if after the price of Y increases to $40, the demand for X falls to 70 units.

Feedback

$CED_{X,Y}$ = (−10/80)/(20/20)

    = −1/8

    = −0.125

Conclusion: the two commodities X and Y are complements.

Conclusion

In this chapter the concept of utility was discussed in detail. The law of diminishing marginal utility was also explained. The concept of consumer equilibrium was addressed using the theory of equimarginal utility as well as indifference curve analysis.

Indifference curve analysis was used to illustrate the income and substitution effects of a price change for various types of goods (normal, inferior and Giffen).

The concept of effective demand was explained within the context of the theory of the demand. The factors affecting demand were also addressed under this discussion. The applied concept of elasticity was discussed.

The concept of consumer surplus was defined and explained.

Key points

- Goods and services are demanded because they provide satisfaction to consumers. Satisfaction in economics is called utility. Utility is therefore the main substantive determinant of demand.
- The total utility that a consumer derives from consuming a good is equitable to the total satisfaction the consumer receives. Marginal utility refers to the satisfaction a consumer receives from consuming *an extra unit* of the commodity.
- The law of diminishing marginal utility infers that as increasing amounts of a commodity are consumed the marginal utility of the additional unit consumed diminishes.
- Using the single commodity situation, the principle of consumer equilibrium can be used to map out the relationship between changes in a commodity's own price and changes in quantity demanded by the consumer.
- An indifference curve is the locus of all the possible of two or more goods, or groups of goods or services, which yield the same level of satisfaction to the consumer.
- An indifference map represents a set of indifference curves, which illustrates the preferences of a consumer.
- The budget line of a consumer shows all the combinations of two goods that a consumer can buy given their relative prices and the consumer's money income.
- If the price of one of the goods entering a consumer's market bundle changes, then the slope of the consumer's budget line will change.
- The consumer is in equilibrium when they maximise the welfare they can obtain subject to the constraints of their income and the market prices of the commodities they purchase. Graphically, consumer equilibrium occurs where the consumer's budget line is just tangential to the highest attainable indifference curve.
- Normal goods in economics are so defined by their relationship with price and consumer income. There is an inverse relationship between quantity demanded and the price, in that as price increases quantity demanded falls and vice versa. With regard to its relationship with income, as consumer income increases, demand for that commodity also increases. In this regard there is a direct relationship between demand and consumer income.
- An inferior good differs from a normal good with respect to its relationship with income. The demand for this type of good actually falls when income rises.
- A Giffen good is a special type of inferior good. The demand for such goods is directly related to their price, such that increases in the market price of a commodity results in an increase in quantity demanded and a decrease in quantity demanded when the market price of the commodity falls.

- There are two types of demand in economics: desired demand and effective demand. Desired demand is an expressed preference for having a particular good or service. Effective demand is desired demand that is 'backed' by the capability to acquire the good or service, that is, effective demand refers to the willingness and the ability to pay for the commodity.

- Desired demand cannot be measured because of the unlimited nature of wants. Effective demand, however, can be measured and, as such, demand in economics is effective rather than desired demand.

- The demand schedule is a tabular representation of the relationship between the price of a commodity and the quantity demanded of it.

- A change in the quantity demanded of a commodity is represented by a movement along the demand curve, while a change in demand is represented by a shift of the demand curve.

- A movement along the curve can either be a contraction or an expansion of quantity demanded and is caused by a change in the price of the commodity. A reduction in price results in an expansion of quantity demanded, while an increase in price results in a contraction of quantity demanded.

- A shift, however, is caused by a change in any of the factors that affect demand other than the commodity's own price. A rightward shift is indicative of an increase in demand, while a leftward shift is indicative of a fall in demand.

- Consumer surplus refers to the benefit obtained by consumers by purchasing a commodity at a particular market price.

- Elasticity is the measure of the responsiveness of the change in one variable to changes in another. Elasticity of demand therefore measures the degree of responsiveness of demand to changes in the factors that affect demand. In economics, we focus on three variables in terms of analysing how these affect demand. These variables are price (in which case the measure is called price elasticity of demand), income (income elasticity of demand) and the price of other goods (cross-elasticity of demand).

3 Theory of supply

Content

- Factors of production: land, labour, capital and entrepreneurship
- Relationship between output and input
- Fixed and variable factors
- The law of diminishing returns
- Calculation of total average and marginal physical product
- Change in the relationship as input increases
- Production and its stages, as they relate to the total, average and marginal product including the use of graphs
- Fixed cost, variable cost, total cost, marginal cost, average fixed cost, average variable cost, average total cost, sunk costs
  - The shape of the long-run average total cost curve
  - Productive optimum
  - The relationship between total, average and marginal cost including the use of graphs
  - Relationship between quantity supplied and price
- Relationship between marginal cost and the average cost in the short run and long run
- Explanation of why the supply curve is the section of the marginal cost curve above the average variable cost and average total cost
- Producer surplus including graphical representations
  - Long run and economies of scale
  - Factors determining economies of scale
  - Internal and external economies of scale
  - Diseconomies of scale
- Returns to scale and the concepts of economies and diseconomies of scale
- Price and the conditions of supply
- Concept of elasticity of supply
- Calculation of elasticity of supply
- Classification and interpretation (size of coefficient) including the drawing and interpretation of graphs

Factors of production: labour, land, capital and entrepreneurial talent

The production of goods and services requires the utilisation of factors of production. Standard economic literature typically identifies four factors of production, specifically land, labour, capital and entrepreneurial talent. In this section we discuss the various factors of production.

Labour

Labour is defined as the human contribution to the production of goods and services, and consists of time and energy spent on producing output.

It includes the actual physical work as well as the mental activities involved in production.

Population and labour force

The population of an economy is important because it forms the basis from which this factor of production is selected. Table 3.1 gives the population figures for the world, developed countries, developing countries and CARICOM. The last two columns show the share of the world population in developed countries as compared to developing countries.

Table 3.1 *Trends in world, developed countries and developing countries population*

Year	World	Developed	Developing	CARICOM	Developed/world	Developing/world
1950	2,556,517,137	863,220,000	1,907,487,000	6,473,138	0.34	0.75
1975	4,086,472,822	1,047,196,000	3,382,413,000	10,144,306	0.26	0.83
1980	4,452,645,562	1,082,539,000	3,762,657,000	10,580,307	0.24	0.85
1985	4,851,854,518	1,114,785,000	4,187,120,000	11,315,587	0.23	0.86
1990	5,282,765,827	1,148,572,000	4,652,763,000	12,054,919	0.22	0.88
1995	5,694,418,460	1,173,983,000	5,115,331,000	12,762,499	0.21	0.90
2000	6,081,527,896	1,193,354,000	5,565,742,000	13,870,177	0.20	0.92

Source: US BUREAU, UN labour statistics

What is clear from Table 3.1 above is that the world population is increasing, and so is the share of the world's population living in developing countries as compared to developed countries. In 1950 the share of the total world population living in developing countries was 75 per cent. This value increased to 92 per cent in 2000. Another factor that influences the labour supply and by extension the workforce is the rate of change in the size of the population. The birth rate and the death rate are two factors to consider, therefore, when addressing changes in the population over time.

Birth and death rates

The population of a country naturally increases because of increases in the birth rate. The birth rate refers to the number of live births per 1,000 of the population. Infant mortality is measured in the same manner and has a negative effect on the growth of the population and the death rate. Table 3.2 below shows this information for Trinidad and Tobago.

Table 3.2 *Trends in birth rate, death rate and infant mortality rate for Trinidad and Tobago*

Year	Birth rate %	Death rate %	Infant mortality rate %
1980	27.61	6.94	18.41
1985	28.62	6.81	11.54
1990	19.50	6.70	12.70

Year	Birth rate %	Death rate %	Infant mortality rate %
1995	15.30	7.20	17.10
2000	na	na	17.00
2001	na	na	na
2002	15.50	6.70	17.00
2003	15.53	6.89	17.00
2004	12.75	na	na

Source: Population and Vital Statistics Report – 1980, 1985, 1990, 1995 (latest edition 1999). UN Common Database – UNICEF, Economic and Social Data Service, World Development Indicators (2005)

In Trinidad and Tobago the birth rate progressively decreased between 1980 and 2004. In 1980 the birth rate was 27.61 per cent, but by 2004 this value fell to 12.75 per cent. Some of the factors influencing this decline in the birth rate may include:

- Improved family planning methods that are more sophisticated and effective and that are more widely available.
- The decision by many households to have a smaller rather than a larger family due to socio-economic and cultural changes.

For Trinidad and Tobago, the data in Table 3.3 gives an indication of the decreasing family size, so that while in 1980 the average size of a household in Trinidad and Tobago was 4.49 persons by 2000 this average fell to 3.64 persons.

Table 3.3 *Trends in average household size for Trinidad and Tobago*

Year	Number of households	Average household size
1980	234,727	4.49
1990	300,816	3.82
2000	343,180	3.64

Source: Population and Housing Census (various years)

There has been a decline in infant mortality rates due to improvements in medical procedures, which has reduced the need to have very large families to ensure that some of the children survive to adulthood.

The general increase in economic welfare of economic agents in Trinidad and Tobago has reduced the need for child labour. Figure 3.1 on page 55 maps out the general inverse relationship between GDP per capita and population growth.

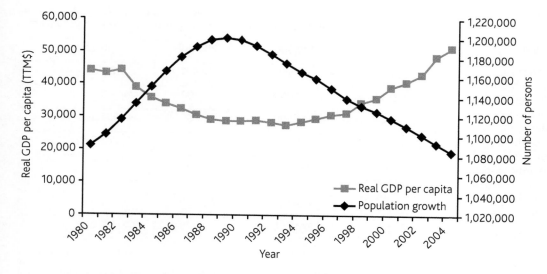

Figure 3.1 *Real GDP per capita (TTM$) and population growth*

Table 3.2 on page 53–4 also illustrates the death rate in Trinidad and Tobago, which has been falling continuously. This falling death rate can be attributed to two main reasons:

■ Declining infant mortality rate (IMR). The IMR measures the number of deaths of children below one year of age per 1,000 of the population. As the infant mortality rate declines, all else remaining constant, then the overall death rate will also decline.

■ Improvements in medicine, hygiene and overall global living standards have also resulted in a general decrease in death rates in Trinidad and Tobago (and most other economies). The increase in the standards of health care coupled with the advances in life-saving technologies has resulted in a greater number of lives being saved.

All of these factors contribute to increasing the population in most economies of the world.

Population density

Table 3.4 indicates the average population density for CARICOM countries. The table shows clearly that Barbados remains the most densely populated economy with Suriname being the most sparsely populated country.

Table 3.4 *Trends in population density in CARICOM*

Country	Population 1999	Area (sq. km)	Persons per sq. km
Antigua and Barbuda	69,747	442	157.80
Bahamas	288,000	13,864	20.77
Barbados	269,350	431	624.94
Belize	240,000	22,966	10.45
Dominica	76,000	750	101.33
Grenada	99,500	345	288.41
Guyana	775,143	214,970	3.61

Example

Thomas Malthus (1766–1834)

Malthus, a political economist educated at Cambridge University, became famous for his contribution to the economic literature on population growth rates. He proposed in his 'Essay on the Principle of Population' (1798) that population grows at an exponential or geometric rate as compared to the earth's ability to sustain itself, which grows only at an arithmetic rate.

Malthus proposed that eventually serious problems (including famines etc.) will occur, as the population growth rate outstrips the rate at which the population can feed itself. Malthus suggested, however, that there are several methods that 'humankind' devises to naturally cut the population size: 'crime, disease, war and vice'. These he indicated as escape valves for the economic pressure being exerted on the world's productive resources.

Malthus also worked in the area of social economics and welfare.

Some of his main publications included *An Inquiry into the Nature and Progress of Rent* (1815, 1970); *Principles of Political Economy* (1820, 1834, 1964); *Definitions in Political Economy* (1827, 1963); *Five Papers on Political Economy by T. R. Malthus*, ed. C. Renwick (1953); *Occasional Papers of T. R. Malthus*, ed. B. Semmel (1963); and *Travel Diaries of T. R. Malthus*, ed. P. James (1966).

Country	Population 1999	Area (sq. km)	Persons per sq. km
Haiti	7,180,000	28,000	256.43
Jamaica	2,540,500	10,991	231.14
Montserrat	5,000	103	48.54
St Kitts and Nevis	42,600	269	158.36
St Lucia	149,621	616	242.89
St Vincent and the Grenadines	111,000	389	285.35
Suriname	418,921	163,820	2.56
Trinidad and Tobago	1,270,000	5,128	247.66

Source: CARICOM (2000), Global Development Finance and World Development Indicators

The Reverend Thomas Malthus, writing in 1798, argued that the global population was growing geometrically, while agriculture was growing arithmetically. In this type of environment, Malthus argued, famine and overt poverty would eventually result in the demise of mankind. To date, Malthus' prediction has not been realised in the intensity in which it was proposed, especially in the more developed countries where technological change in agriculture has reduced any prospect of critical food shortages. However, in some parts of the world, agricultural growth does not appear to be outstripping the growth of the population (in Africa), in which case Malthus' argument may yet carry some weight.

Size of the workforce

In the CARICOM sphere (as in most other economies), there are a number of factors that condition the segment of the population that enters the workforce. These may include:

- Retirement: although in practice the workforce excludes people above 64 years, many of these people remain in the workforce via part-time work, contract or consultancy work with their former employers. In conducting assessments of the labour force, people over 64 years are treated as 'not in the labour force'.

- Education: a significant part of the population in the age group 16–24 years is enrolled in educational programmes. CARICOM has issued a mandate to increase to 15 per cent the relevant segment of CARICOM populations in the age cohort 16–24 years that are enrolled in tertiary level education. This will no doubt influence the size of the labour force, as there will be a greater tendency for people to enter the workforce at a later rather than an earlier age.

- Institutionalisation: in the age group 16–64 years, some people may be institutionalised (e.g. in hospitals or in prison etc.) and will not form part of the labour force.

- Role of women: in developing economies in particular, a significant influencing factor on the size of the workforce is the number of women entering the workforce. Traditionally women were viewed as homemakers and caregivers. This view has been slowly changing within CARICOM economies, resulting in a greater number of women entering the labour force today as compared to previous years.

Figure 3.2 shows that there has been a steady increase in the percentage of women in the workforce.

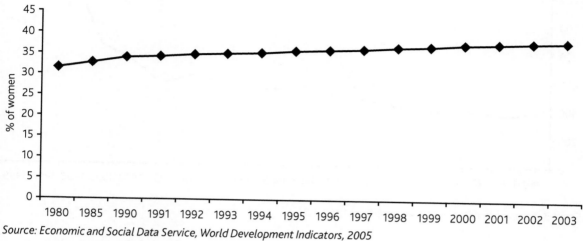

Source: Economic and Social Data Service, World Development Indicators, 2005

Figure 3.2 Percentage of women in the Trinidad and Tobago workforce

A significant influence on total labour effort is also the number of hours worked by the employed part of the labour force, where:

Total labour effort = Number of workers × Average numbers of hours worked

This implies that as the number of hours worked increases, all else remaining constant, the total contribution of labour to production increases.

An equally important factor is the quality of the labour force. In general, the higher the quality of the labour force, the better poised the country is to sustainably pursue growth and development strategies.

Entrepreneurial talent

The entrepreneur refers to the factor of production that combines all the other factors of production in the productive process. In the past, the entrepreneur carried a heavy responsibility including taking all the risks, providing all the capital and making all the key decisions.

Today, given the extent of the growth of large firms in most economies, the role of the entrepreneur has been superseded by the role of management. As such, there exists the perception that management is a particular type of labour contribution. In this scenario, management can also be regarded as entrepreneurship, which is the factor of production responsible for the organisation of productive resources in the production function.

As a proxy of entrepreneurial talent the number of graduates from the University of the West Indies is used in figure 3.3 on page 58. It is clear from this graph that the number of graduates have been increasing continually over the period, indicating that the stock of tertiary educated individuals is increasing.

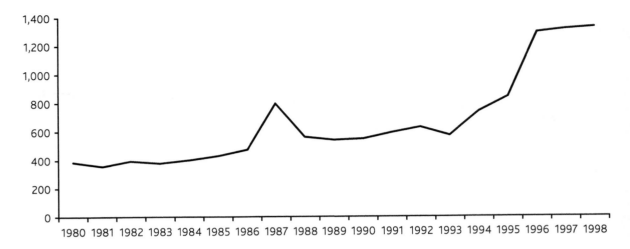

Figure 3.3 *University of the West Indies graduates 1980–98*

In addition, if it is assumed that each member of the labour force contributes at least 25 years in service, then the entrepreneurial environment is increased every year as the stock of entrepreneurial talent increases.

Capital

Classical economists regard capital as those commodities that are man-made and used in the production of other goods and services. David Ricardo later amended this definition to include what is known as circulating capital, such as intermediate goods or raw materials, which are required for the operations of a firm.

Capital can be found in a number of varied forms, including:

- Stocks of producer goods: these include machinery and buildings etc. Thus a bauxite company in Jamaica may keep in store two drill bits or two piles of dynamite for blasting purposes.
- Stocks of raw materials (circulating capital): firms keep these stocks to produce final commodities at short notice without interruptions.

In classical economics, investment was regarded as the means of improving the capital stock. Investment in this regard requires that savings be accumulated. Consumers can either consume their income or save it. When resources are saved it provides a pool from which investments can be made.

Savings ⟶ Financial intermediaries ⟶ Investment

In modern economics the definition of capital has been broadened to include the following:

- Financial capital: the liquid monetary assets of economic agents.
- Natural capital: the assets of nature, for example natural resources.
- Infrastructural capital: the man-made facilities that support and enable production. These include buildings, fixtures, ports and road networks.
- Human capital: the rewards arising out of investments in skills and education.

■ Social capital: the investment that enhances the network of relationships existing between individuals within society. These include investments in health care, education, preventing crime, etc.

Table 3.5 shows the level of investment in social capital, or rather, investments into those plans and programmes that are geared towards the improvement of the social capital stock of the Trinidad and Tobago economy.

Table 3.5 *Expenditure on social programmes, 2003*

Programme	Estimated expenditure TT$
DEVELOPMENTAL PROGRAMMES	
Human development	300,563,098
Poverty alleviation	2,924,726
Social integration	15,564,869
Community development and empowerment	257,591,486
Sustainable livelihoods	25,806,675
REMEDIAL PROGRAMMES	
Poverty alleviation	961,074,821
Human development	586,390
Social integration	4,659,780
Personal safety and security	240,000
Community development and empowerment	15,792,200
PREVENTIVE PROGRAMMES	
Poverty alleviation	293,334,439
Human development	205,477
Wellness and well-being	24,205,000
Personal safety and security	1,646,230

Source: Social Sector Investment Program (2004)

Capital formation: gross capital formation

Capital formation refers to the extent to which the capital stock is increased annually.

The capital stock (K) is augmented by investment. Thus:

$$K_t = K_{t-1} + I_t$$

This says that capital stock today (K_t) is the same as the capital stock yesterday (K_{t-1}) plus investment today (I_t).

Gross capital formation is a measure of net new investments into the domestic economy. Gross capital formation is a flow concept that estimates the total addition to the existing stock of capital. Gross capital formation includes gross fixed capital formation, investments in intangible assets, such as intellectual property, as well as financial investments.

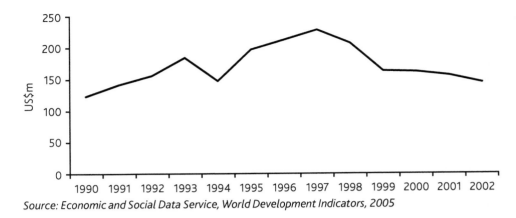

Source: Economic and Social Data Service, World Development Indicators, 2005

Figure 3.4 *Gross capital formation in Guyana (US$million), 1990–2002*

Figure 3.4 gives a snapshot of the extent of the gross capital formation of a Caribbean country.

Foreign direct investment is an important contributor to the capital formation process in all CARICOM economies.

Human capital formation

Human capital is regarded as a factor of production for several reasons. In particular, human capital in the form of ideas and knowledge has several characteristics that are peculiar only to this factor of production. Firstly, knowledge is non-rivalrous and secondly it is non-diminishing, which means that human capital has the potential to utilise cumulative ideas and as such further the rate of technological innovation and hence economic growth.

Table 3.6 shows the percentage of the primary-school enrolment ratio for the period 1990–96 and 1996–2002 for several Caribbean countries. From this table it can be concluded that a relatively high rate of literacy exists in these various economies.

Table 3.6 *Primary-school enrolment ratio CARICOM, 1990–2002*

	1990–96	1996–2002
Anguilla	–	–
Antigua and Barbuda	100	98
Bahamas, The	100	83
Barbados	90	100
Belize	121	100
Dominica	–	89
Dominican Republic	103	93
Grenada	88	84
Guyana	95	87
Haiti	56	54

Jamaica	107	95
Martinique	–	–
Montserrat	–	–
Saint Kitts and Nevis	–	89
Saint Lucia	95	100
Saint Vincent and the Grenadines	95	84
Suriname	127	92
Trinidad and Tobago	96	92

Source: World Health Organization, World Health Report 1999 and The State of the World's Children 2004

Note: *The primary-school enrolment ratio is derived by dividing the number of children in primary schools by the number of children who are in the age group who would normally attend primary schools.*

Land

Land refers to the resources provided by nature and includes mineral deposits, wind and wave power, as well as solar power. Land, in its literal sense, is generally regarded as being fixed in supply. However, with the development of modern technologies this resource is being more efficiently exploited resulting in an expansion in the potential of this resource to contribute to production. Table 3.7 below shows the physical land acreage in CARICOM economies.

Table 3.7 *Land area for CARICOM countries, 2000*

Country	Area (sq. km)
Antigua and Barbuda	442
Bahamas	13,864
Barbados	431
Belize	22,966
Dominica	750
Grenada	345
Guyana	214,970
Haiti*	28,000
Jamaica	10,991
Montserrat	103
St Kitts and Nevis	269
St Lucia	616
St Vincent and the Grenadines	389

Table 3.8 *Mineral deposits in selected Caribbean countries*

BAHAMAS, THE	
Salt	Stone, aragonite

BARBADOS	
Clay and shale Limestone	Sand

CUBA	
Asphalt	Kaolin clay
Chromate	Lime
Cobalt, mine output, Co content	Nickel, Ni content: Crue
Feldspar	Salt
Gold	Sand
Gypsum	Silica sand
Iron and steel, steel, crude	

SAINT KITTS AND NEVIS	
Sand and gravel	Stone, crushed

TRINIDAD AND TOBAGO	
Asphalt, natural	Natural gas

Source: USGS Minerals Information

Example

Natural gas find in Trinidad and Tobago

Technological advances in geology have facilitated the extraction of more crude oil from any given oil field, for example, with the new commercial find by BHP Billiton on a previously explored bloc. No discoveries were made before and as such the ownership of the bloc was relinquished to the GOTT. BHP Billiton, after successful bidding, acquired the same bloc and proceeded to explore using new technologies and equipment.

The size of the commercial find is estimated according to some officials at 1 billion barrels of crude oil.

Country	Area (sq. km)
Suriname	163,820
Trinidad and Tobago	5,128

Notes: *Provisional member

Source: CARICOM (2000). Global Development Finance and World Development Indicators

Examples of ways in which natural resources enter into the production function include:

- It is one of the most significant of all the factors of production conditioning agricultural output.
- It provides a physical location for manufacturing industries and tertiary-level activities. Thus an ammonia plant will need a physical location, even as the establishment of a university will also require a physical location. In modern times, given concerns over pollution, governments have to practice land allocation so that pollutants and wastes from factories do not significantly affect residential uses of land. Some land is also deployed for recreational use.

The waterways of the world provide significant opportunities for food and energy production. For example, in the rivers of Guyana large amounts of fish are caught and sold on the market. In addition to this, there is also the potential to use hydro-electric power.

In 2002 the ENMAN Engineering Services Ltd, an engineering company based in Trinidad and Tobago, signed a memorandum of understanding with the government of Guyana to develop a hydroelectric power plant in Guyana. (Guyana-Turtruba Hydro/Aluminium Project. Project Profile. http://enmangroup.com)

Many CARICOM economies also extract valuable minerals from the earth, either for domestic use or for export to foreign markets.

Table 3.8 shows some of the mineral deposits that exist in some CARICOM countries.

Although land is generally fixed in supply, it can fluctuate up or down for the following reasons:

- Land reclamation from the sea.
- Irrigation of formerly arid lands.
- Draining waterlogged lands.
- Technological advancement; new techniques to extract more resources from 'land'.
- Erosion of hillsides. Many of the Caribbean islands have steep topographies. This, coupled with poor soil and watershed management, often results in landsides along these hillsides.
- Weather. Land supply can decrease through abuse or adverse weather conditions. For example, in Belize the strong winds from storm surges damage the Belizean coast to the extent that barriers have to be erected along the coastline.

The theory of production

The theory of production refers to the study of the relationship between factor inputs and output. That is, it is a study of the changes in output when the amounts of factors of production utilised are varied in the production process. In this regard, therefore, it is necessary to first define some of the concepts associated with this theory.

- A factor input refers to any good or service that is used to produce output.
- Factor inputs are classified as either being fixed or variable.
- A fixed input is one that remains constant over the period of production, that is, it does not vary with the level of output produced.
- A variable input is one that is directly related to the level of output produced.
- The short-run period refers to that period over which at least one factor input is held constant, that is, there is at least one fixed factor used in the production of output. In many cases this factor is either land or capital. For the rest of this chapter capital is assumed to be the fixed factor input, with labour being the variable input.
- The long-run period is defined as that period of time over which all factors of production are variable but the state of technology remains unchanged. The long run is known as the planning horizon of the firm.

The production function

The production function refers to a technically efficient combination of factor inputs that, when fed into the production process, gives a particular level of output. A typical production function can be expressed as below:

$$Q^n_t = Q[f_1 \dots f_m]_t$$

where

Q^n_t is the quantity of the commodity n that is produced in the given time period

Q is the production process that is conditioned by the level of technology

$f_1 \dots f_m$ are the m factors of production used to produce the commodity n.

Any given production function can be examined in either the short or the long run. As alluded to above, in the short run, at least one factor of production is held fixed, while in the long run all factor inputs are variable. The functions below express this difference:

$$Q^n_t = Q(L,K)_t \qquad \text{the long run}$$
$$Q^n_t = Q(L, \grave{\overline{K}})_t \qquad \text{the short run}$$

where

L is labour

K is capital

The change from 'K' to '$\grave{\overline{K}}$' indicates a change in the availability of the factor from being readily available, K, or variable, to being fixed, '$\grave{\overline{K}}$'.

The short-run production period

In the short run, increases in output can only be achieved by increasing the variable factor of production. Some important concepts associated with the short-run production horizon are explained below.

Total product of a variable factor (TPL)

Total product refers to the total output produced by a firm at a given level of capital and labour employment. The total output of the firm

Example
Hillside soil erosion in St Lucia

In September 1994 tropical storm Debbie produced rainfall intensities that reached as high as 125 mm/hr in St Lucia. The rainfall from the storm coupled with the steep topography and agricultural production on the sloping lands led to severe soil erosion. There was little by way of soil conservation measures and 'slash and burn agriculture' was predominantly practised, exacerbating the effects of the storm. Traditionally, farmers throughout the Windward Islands have been clearing trees and moving into the upper extremities of catchments on very steep and fragile slopes to build houses and plant crops such as bananas. This practice, however, is characteristic of many Caribbean countries. It has resulted in the loss of valuable tree species and exposed wide expanses of hillside lands during the high rainfall periods. The result has been landslides which have blocked waterways and roads and destroyed crops and private property.

will therefore be directly related to the level of employment of labour, as labour is assumed to be the only variable factor. In this case the change in total product, as a result of a change in the level of employment of labour, is given by:

$$\Delta Q = f(\Delta L)$$

where 'Δ' means change.

Average product of labour (APL)

The average product of labour is the per unit output of a labourer, given fixed capital inputs.

This value can be obtained using the following formula:

$$AP_L = TP_L/L$$

where L is the number of workers. TP_L is the total output of the firm employing L workers.

Marginal product of labour (MPL)

The marginal product of labour refers to the change in the total output of the firm that results from the employment of the last unit of labour. The marginal product of labour is therefore the amount of output that each additional labourer produces.

If TP_L represents the total output that L labourers produce and TP_{L+1} is the corresponding output for L + 1 labourers, then the output of the (L + 1)th labourer is given by:

$$MP_{(L+1)} = TP_{L+1} - TP_L$$

The relationship between TP, AP and MP

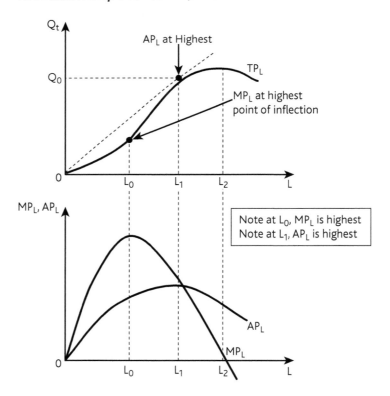

Figure 3.5 *The relationship between TP$_L$, AP$_L$ and MP$_L$*

Figure 3.5 on page 64 illustrates the relationship between the various product curves. Observe that the MP_L reaches a peak at L_0 workers and subsequently decreases. On the TP_L curve this occurs at the point of inflection. Similarly the AP_L curve increases until L_1 workers are employed but thereafter decreases. On the TP curve this corresponds to the point of tangency between a ray from the origin and the TP curve. The marginal product of the firm decreases between the L_0 and L_1 workers, whilst at the same time the AP_L increases. Even though the MP_L is decreasing in the zone L_0 to L_1 workers, the MP_L is still higher than the average product such that it follows:

$$AP_L \text{ increases if } MP_L > AP_L$$
$$AP_L \text{ decreases if } MP_L < AP_L$$
$$AP_L \text{ is constant if } MP_L = AP_L$$

The stages of production

Figure 3.6 decomposes the production of the firm into three substantive stages of production. The first stage of production occurs up to the point where the AP curve is at its maximum. The second stage of production occurs between the points where AP is at its highest and where MP is zero. The third stage of production occurs when MP becomes negative.

The producer will in general operate in stage 2. This is because in stage 1 the AP of labour is increasing and therefore it is feasible for the firm to continue production. In stage 3 the output of the firm is actually falling so it makes sense for the firm to cut back production in this stage. Stage 2 therefore represents the optimum production stage for the producer.

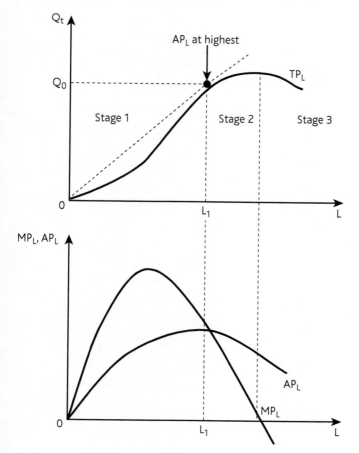

Figure 3.6 *The stages of production*

Activity 3.1

Calculate the total and the average productivity from the following information.

Plot the total productivity curve as well as the marginal and the average productivity curves.

Number of workers	Marginal product
1	5.0
2	8.0
3	12.0
4	14.0
5	13.5
6	12.0
7	10.0
8	8.0
9	5.0
10	3.5
11	1.5
12	0.0

Feedback

Number of workers	Marginal product	TP_L	AP_L
1	5.0	5.0	5.0
2	8.0	13.0	6.5
3	12.0	25.0	8.3
4	14.0	39.0	9.8
5	13.5	52.5	10.5
6	12.0	64.5	10.8
7	10.0	74.5	10.6
8	8.0	82.5	10.3
9	5.0	87.5	9.7
10	3.5	91.0	9.1
11	1.5	92.5	8.4
12	0.0	92.5	7.7

Figure 3.7 *The total product of labour*

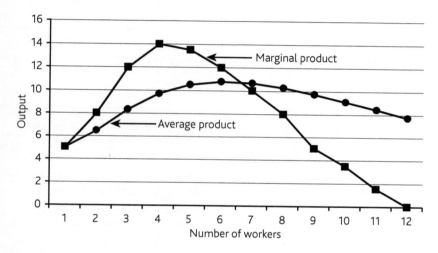

Figure 3.8 *The relationship between average and marginal product*

The law of diminishing marginal returns/law of variable proportions

The short-run production schedule shows that as increasing quantities of a variable factor are utilised in association with a given amount of a fixed factor, the returns to the variable factor eventually decrease.

This describes the 'law of diminishing marginal returns', also known as the 'law of variable proportions'. This law has real implications for any business venture particularly in relation to the per-unit cost of production. This section is devoted to providing a clearer and more meaningful explanation of this important concept.

In the short run, we have

$$Q_1 = f(L, \overline{K})$$

where Q_1 is the output level associated with L units of labour.

Let p and m represent the change in input of the variable factor and the output levels of the commodity respectively, so that

$$mQ_1 = f(pL, \overline{K})$$

where mQ_1 is the output level associated with pL workers.

If

$$p < m$$

then the short-run production function exhibits increasing returns to the variable factor because output increases at a faster proportional rate than the factor input. If

$$p > m$$

the short-run production function exhibits decreasing returns to the variable factor, because output increases at a slower rate than factor inputs and if

$$p = m$$

the short-run production function exhibits constant returns to the variable factor.

Activity 3.2

Discuss of the reasons why marginal product may rise or fall.

Feedback

The law of diminishing returns states that as additional amounts of a variable factor are applied to a fixed factor, first the marginal, then the average and finally the total product will fall.

Consider a farm situation, where the fixed factor of production is land and the variable factor is labour. Initially the output of the land is nil, but as labour is hired the output of the land will begin to increase. As more workers are hired, output will continue to rise as work will be divided up among the labourers. Both the marginal and the average productivity of labour will rise.

However, as more units of labour are hired, the rate of increase in output will begin to fall and eventually total output of the farm will also fall. This is the law of diminishing returns in practice. The factors that may initially cause the marginal productivity of workers to increase would include division of labour where, as more workers are employed, work can be shared, which allows for specialisation and increased efficiency hence resulting in increased output per worker. Over time, however, the output per worker will eventually fall. This fall in marginal productivity may be due to 'over-manning' of a particular task, where the work environment itself becomes to clustered, resulting in a fall in the productivity per worker. Marginal productivity may also fall due to poor management of variable resources.

The theory of cost and supply

Introduction

As with the theory of production discussed earlier in this chapter, costs can be discussed in the short as well as in the long run. Costs are a function of the level of inputs employed in the production process. Consider the two equations below which represent costs in the long run (1) and in the short run (2) respectively:

$$C = F(Q, T, P_f)$$
$$C = F(Q, T, P_f, \bar{K})$$

where

C: total cost

Q: output

T: technology

P_f: factor prices

$\overline{K}$: fixed factors of production, most commonly, capital.

The equations above represent the cost function of a firm in the long and short run respectively. Note that in the second equation there is the element K, which represents the fixed factor of capital. Fixed factors of production are characteristic of short-run production functions because of the fact that firms are unable to significantly change their scale of production in the short run, but are able to vary all their factors in the long run.

Short-run costs

- Total fixed costs (TFC): although the input of some factors of production may be flexible, in the short run, not all factor inputs can be modified. The cost of employing such fixed factor inputs into the production process of the firm represents its total fixed costs. Typical examples of fixed costs to a firm include rent, salaries for administrative staff, or interest on loans.

- Total variable cost (TVC): the total variable costs of a firm refers to the costs incurred by the firm to employ its variable factors of production in the short run. If we treat wages (w) as the price of labour then the total variable costs of the firm that employs L workers is:

$$TVC = wL$$

- Total cost (TC): the cost of producing a particular level of output is the sum of total fixed costs (TFC) and total variable costs (TVC).

$$TC = TVC + TFC$$

Figure 3.9 shows the relationship between total fixed and total variable costs and total costs.

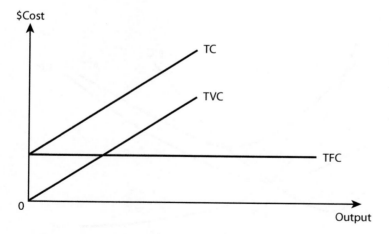

Figure 3.9 *Short-run total cost curves*

- Marginal cost: the incremental or extra cost a firm incurs in producing the last unit of output. Algebraically, the marginal cost of producing the nth unit of output can be derived from:

$$MC_{n\text{th}} = TC_n - TC_{n-1}$$

where

MC_{nth} is the marginal cost of the nth unit

TC_n is the TC of the nth unit

TC_{n-1} is the TC of the $n - 1$ unit.

That is, if the total cost of producing $n - 1$ and n units is TC_{n-1} and TC_n respectively, the difference between these two cost levels represent the marginal cost of producing the nth unit of output.

The short-run average total cost (SRATC) indicates the cost per unit of producing a particular level of output. The SRATC is obtained by dividing the total costs of producing a particular level of output by this level of output. For example, if the firm produces X_1 units of a commodity at a total cost of TC_{X1}, then the average cost per unit of this output is:

$$ATC_{X1} = TC_{X1}/X_1$$

- Average variable cost (AVC): the average variable cost of producing a particular level of output is the total variable cost of producing this particular level of output divided by the number of units produced. Thus if the firm produces X_2 units of a commodity at a total variable cost of TVC_{X2} then the average variable cost of producing these X_2 units of output is given as:

$$AVC_{X2} = TVC_{Z2}/X_2$$

- Average fixed cost (AFC): the average fixed cost of producing a particular quantity of output is determined by dividing the total fixed costs (which remain unchanged) by that quantity of output. Thus if the firm produces X_2 units of a commodity at a total fixed cost of TFC_{X2}, then the average fixed cost of producing these X_2 units of output is given as:

$$AFC_{X2} = TFC_{X2}/X_2$$

Figure 3.10 below shows the relationship between average cost, average variable cost, average fixed cost and marginal cost.

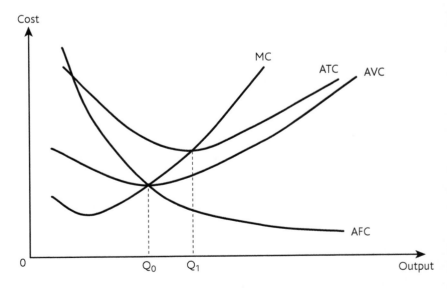

Figure 3.10 *Short-run average and marginal cost curves*

Activity 3.3

The table below gives the total cost, total variable cost and total fixed cost curves of a firm engaged in producing copybooks. Calculate the marginal and average costs associated with production. Draw the corresponding total and per unit average cost curves.

Q	TFC	TVC	TC
0	40	0	40
1	40	15	55
2	40	25	65
3	40	30	70
4	40	40	80
5	40	55	95
6	40	80	120
7	40	120	160
8	40	180	220

Feedback

Q	TFC	TVC	TC	MC	AFC	AVC	ATC
0	40	0	40				
1	40	15	55	15	40	15	55
2	40	25	65	10	20	13	33
3	40	30	70	5	13	10	23
4	40	40	80	10	10	10	20
5	40	55	95	15	8	11	19
6	40	80	120	25	7	13	20
7	40	120	160	40	6	17	23
8	40	180	220	60	5	23	28

Note that the total variable cost curve of the firm starts at the origin as with zero level of output the firm incurs zero variable costs. The total fixed cost curve is a horizontal straight line indicating that, regardless of the level of output of the firm, the total fixed costs of the firm do not change. The total cost curve of the firm is simply a lateral summation of the total variable cost curve and the total fixed cost curve of the firm.

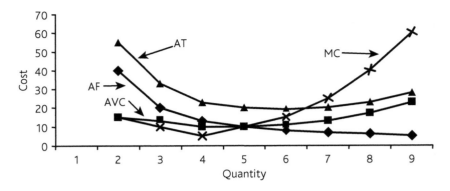

Figure 3.11 *Marginal cost and average costs*

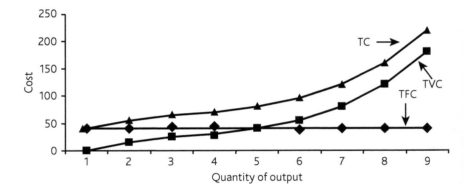

Figure 3.12 *Total cost curves*

The shape of the average total cost curves

Normal average total cost curves (ATC) are U-shaped. The shape of this curve is due primarily to the principles and laws upon which the two components of average cost are based.

As discussed on page 70, average total cost can be calculated as average total cost divided by the number of units produced. An alternative method of calculating average total cost is to sum the individual values of average variable and average fixed costs for a given quantity of output.

$$ATC = AFC + AVC$$

The average fixed cost curve slopes downward from left to right continually without ever reaching zero. This is because output increases but fixed costs remain unchanged over the scale of operations ($AFC = TFC/X$). The shape of the average fixed cost curve therefore is that of a rectangular hyperbola.

The average variable cost curve on the other hand is U-shaped. The falling portion of the average variable cost curve reflects an improvement in the use of the available resources due to specialisation and division of labour. However, the rising portion of the average variable cost curve is reflective of the law of diminishing marginal returns. This law, discussed on page 70, states that as continuous amounts of a variable factor of production are combined with a given amount of another factor of production, the marginal productivity and average productivity of the firm will fall. The falling productivity of factors corresponds to rising variable cost as shown below.

Considering Figure 3.13 below, observe that the average cost curve of the firm is a vertical summation of the average fixed and average variable cost curves.

Over the range a–b, the ATC curve is falling; this is due to the fact that both the AFC and AVC curves are falling. Over the range b–c, the ATC continues to fall in spite of the fact that the AVC curve is beginning to rise over this range. This occurs because the rise in AVC is offset by the fall in AFC. Beyond point c, however, the fall in AFC can no longer compensate for the rise in AVC, so the ATC curve begins to rise. The AVC curve therefore reaches its minimum before the ATC curve.

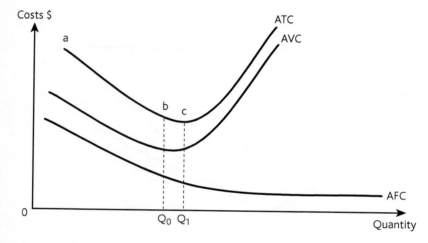

Figure 3.13 *The shape of the average cost curve*

Example

Sunk costs

Sunk costs are incurred by a business and cannot necessarily be recovered to any great extent. For example, if a person prepays for movie tickets, whether that individual decides to go to the movies or not, the cost has already been incurred and as such cannot be recovered.

The same principle is applied at company level. For example, if a firm invests in a building, the costs incurred in the construction of that building are sunk, in that funds have already been spent on the project.

Cost and production

Cost and productivity are related concepts in that costs are incurred in the production process. Figure 3.14 shows the relationship between the per unit productivity curves and the per unit cost curves.

Figure 3.14 also shows that as the marginal productivity of workers increases, the marginal cost of production falls. This is obvious as variable costs are being spread over a greater amount of output. A similar rationale applies to the relationship between average productivity and average variable cost. As marginal productivity begins to fall, however, marginal costs rise. Also as average productivity falls, average variable cost rises.

From Figure 3.14 therefore it can be shown that the highest point of the marginal productivity curve corresponds to the lowest point of the marginal cost curve. Also the highest point of the average productivity curve corresponds to the lowest point of the average variable cost curve.

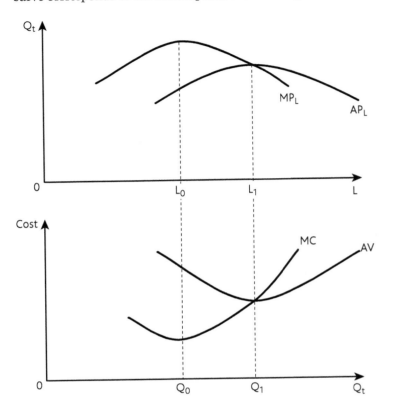

Figure 3.14 *Relationship between short-run production and cost curves*

The long-run cost curve

In the short run, the input of at least one factor of production is fixed, while in the long run the inputs of all factors of production are variable. The relationship between short-run and long-run cost curves can be expressed in Figure 3.15.

Let SAC_0 represent the initial short-run average total cost curve. As the market demand for the output of this firm increases it will need to build larger plants, for example it can build a plant such as that represented by SAC_1. As the market size grows, the firm can proceed to a larger-sized plant corresponding to SAC_2. However, in the context of the prevailing technology, even if the firm were to build larger and larger plants, eventually all possible benefits of size (economies of scale) would become exhausted and the firm, on expanding onto a plant such as that represented by SAC_2, will be characterised by significant inefficiencies (diseconomies of scale). Simply put, there are certain plant sizes beyond which the short-run average per unit costs rise as the firm expands. All possible short-run plant sizes, represented by the short-run average costs curves, are enveloped by the long-run average cost (LAC) curve. The LAC is therefore called the envelope curve.

As can be seen in Figure 3.15, the long-run average cost curve is U-shaped. This shape is influenced by economies and diseconomies of scale, concepts that will be dealt with next.

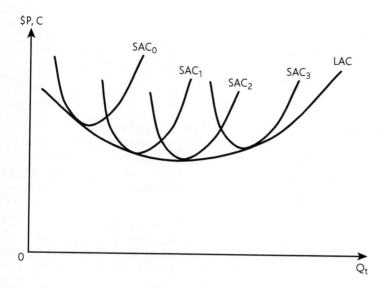

Figure 3.15 *Long run average cost curve*

The long run: increasing returns to scale

Consider the generic production function below

$$mQ_t = f(pL, pK)$$

where m is proportionate expansion in the production of the output of the firm and p is the proportionate expansion in all factor inputs.

There are three possible permutations between m and p:

$m > p$: increasing returns to *scale*

$m = p$: constant returns to *scale*

$m < p$: decreasing returns to *scale*

Firms experience two principal types of economies of scale: those arising from activities of the firm itself (internal economies of scale) and those arising from activities of the industry within which the firm operates (external economies of scale).

Figure 3.16 gives the ranges over which increasing, constant and decreasing returns to scale occur in the long run.

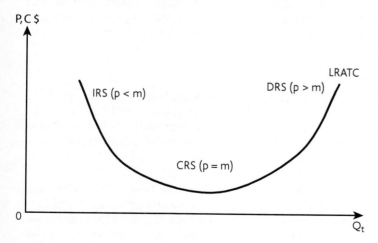

Figure 3.16 *Phases in the long run*

Internal economies of scale

Economies of scale refer to the benefits derived by increasing the scale of operations of a firm. There are several factors that account for internal economies of scale, these are as follows.

Technical economies

Large firms can employ specialists. Small private universities, for example, sometimes use one economist to teach international economics, microeconomics and macroeconomics, while in large universities these activities are carried out by separate specialists. As workers specialise, the productivity in their various areas of strength becomes higher and so the overall output of the firm increases.

With large firms, machinery is more efficiently utilised. In small firms, given their market size, it may not be possible to use a machine intensively and so some of the machines' operating time on a daily basis may remain idle. With large firms, machines are more likely to be fully utilised and so associated operational costs are low.

There are also benefits that accrue to physical increases in size. For example, if a container doubles in size, its area quadruples while its volume expands eightfold. This implies that in the case where these containers are used as storage, cost per unit falls significantly as the size of the unit increases.

Larger firms are also capable of undertaking extensive amounts of research and development (R&D), which can facilitate an overall reduction in production costs. R&D allows for innovation and development of new and improved technologies, the costs for which are spread over a larger number of units, so that R&D is more cost-effective at a larger rather than at a smaller scale of operations.

Management economies

When a firm expands its scale of output, it most commonly remains with a single chief executive officer and board of directors. Thus as a firm expands, the managerial cost per unit of running the firm will decline, all else remaining constant.

Market economies

When firms are large, they typically buy their factor inputs in bulk and so can negotiate for lower production costs. Lowered transportation costs are also a benefit under market economies where, as greater amounts of goods enter into the transactions between a firm and particular shipping company, for example, the firm will generally benefit through the realisation of lower per unit costs.

Financial economies

Large firms usually benefit from established relations with financial intermediaries and, because of their greater demand for financial resources, they may be offered better repayment options. Larger firms will also typically have more collateral to hold as security against loans.

Risk-bearing economies

Larger and more established firms may have the benefit of a wider spread of output so that even if the price of one of its products falls, it will not necessarily carry an exceptional financial burden. Larger firms may also purchase raw materials from more than one supplier and so may be able to safeguard their operation against default by one of its suppliers.

External economies of scale

Better training

Better training facilities reduce the overall costs to the industry, in that the firms operating in that industry have a larger pool of trained individuals from which to source labour. In addition to this, the firms themselves do not have to engage in training of labour and as such this would mean that firms face lower costs throughout the industry.

Better transportation

Similarly, better transport facilities benefit the industry as a whole, by reducing the time taken for raw materials to be delivered, for example, or for goods to be delivered to the markets. Better transportation facilities have the effect of reducing overall company costs for each firm in the industry as the firm does not have to engage in this activity itself.

Better commercial services

Commercial services refer to the support services that every company, and by extension an industry, requires in order to interact with its suppliers and customers. Better commercial support services of this type will make market interaction a much less difficult process and will hence reduce the cost of production for the individual firm and so the industry as a whole.

Diseconomies of scale

Diseconomies of scale refer to the disadvantages of increases in the scale of operations. Diseconomies of scale can also be addressed in terms of internal and external diseconomies of scale.

The main reason why internal diseconomies arise is that of bureaucracy. Managerial inefficiencies and red tape may arise as the organisation itself becomes larger. This has the effect of slowing productivity and hence increasing long-run average costs.

External diseconomies of scale can arise out of situations where firms in the industry engage in intense competition for the available resources, in which case costs of these resources increase and hence the overall costs to the industry. External diseconomies also arise when the industry itself pollutes the environment and so on.

L-shaped cost curves

There are certain long-run supply conditions for which the overall per unit costs do not change or rather do not change significantly with an increase in the scale of production. These industries or firms face a long-run average cost curve that is L-shaped. Examples of such industries include the newspaper industry and the bottled water industry.

The L-shaped long-run supply curve is therefore representative of a situation of constant returns to scale where for a given increase in size there is a proportional increase in production and hence per unit costs remain constant. A diagrammatic representation of this type of scenario is shown in Figure 3.17.

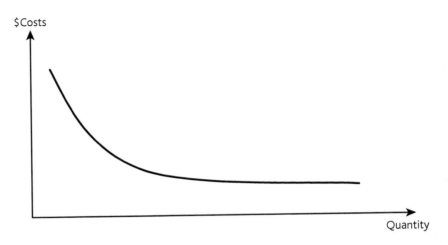

Figure 3.17 *Long-run average total cost curve*

Attainable and unattainable costs

Considering the LRAC curve in Figure 3.18, a point such as B is unattainable in the context of the available technology, while a point such as A is certainly attainable but represents inefficient levels of production.

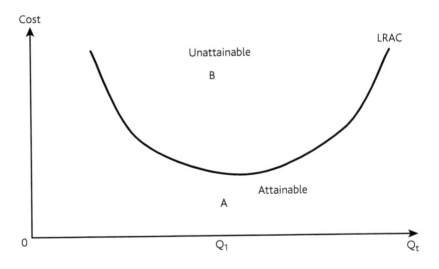

Figure 3.18 *Attainable and unattainable costs*

The theory of supply

Supply refers to the amount of a commodity that is brought to the market at a particular price over a specific period of time. For example, the supply of tomatoes may be quoted as 100 pounds per week at a price of $5.00 per pound.

The supply function can be expressed as

$$Qs = Tf(P, P_0, P_f, G, \theta)$$

where

T: state of technology

P: price of commodity

P_0: price of other commodities

P_f: price of factors of production

G: goals of the firm

θ: all other factors

As with demand, the simple supply function, which describes the relationship between price and quantity supplied, can be represented by a table, in which case it is referred to as a supply schedule (see Table 3.9).

The graphical representation of the supply schedule is called the supply curve. The relationship between price and quantity supplied is a positive or direct one where, as prices increase, all else remaining constant, the quantity supplied will also increase.

Movements along and shifts of the supply curves

A movement along the supply curve is caused by changes in the commodity's own market price. Movements along the supply curve, as along the demand curve, are called extensions and contractions of quantity supplied. An increase in price results in an extension or increase in quantity supplied, while a reduction in price results in a contraction or decrease in quantity supplied.

Figure 3.19 below shows movements along the supply curve.

Table 3.9 *Supply schedule*

Prices of crab	Quantity supplied of crab
1	3
2	5
3	7
4	15
5	18
6	22
7	26
8	31
9	39
10	47

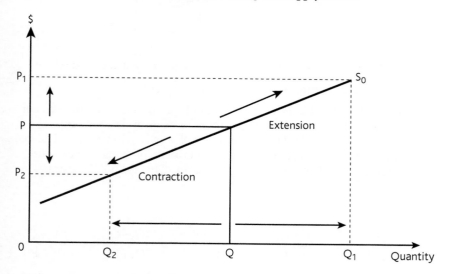

Figure 3.19 *Movements along the supply curve*

Changes in the non-price factors that affect supply result in a change in supply rather than a change in the quantity supplied. A change in supply is evidenced by shift of the supply curve, either rightward or leftward (see figure 3.20).

If changes in the environment result in increased willingness of suppliers to supply a product then the supply curve shifts rightward. However, if changes in the environment result in a diminished willingness to supply a product then the supply curve shifts leftwards.

Shifts are therefore the result of changes in any of the non-price factors that affect supply.

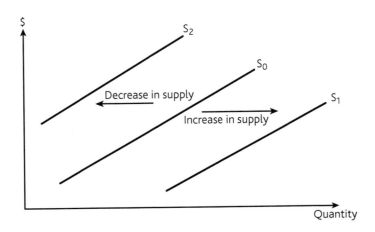

Figure 3.20 *Shifts of the supply curve*

Elasticity of supply

Price elasticity of supply measures the responsiveness of quantity supplied to changes in the commodity's own price. Elasticity of supply is calculated as

$$ES = \frac{\%\Delta Q_s^n}{\%\Delta P_n}$$

where

$\%\Delta Q_s^n$: Percentage change in quantity supplied of a particular good n

$\%\Delta P_n$: Percentage change in the price of n.

Elasticity of supply, like elasticity of demand, can be discussed in terms of a particular point or over a particular range. The formula above gives the point elasticity of supply. The arc elasticity of supply, however, is calculated using the same formula as that of the arc elasticity of demand, but with supply rather than demand values for quantity. This formula is given as

$$PES = \frac{\left(\dfrac{Q_2-Q_1}{\dfrac{Q_2+Q_1}{2}}\right)}{\dfrac{P_2-P_1}{\dfrac{P_2+P_1}{2}}} = \frac{Q_2-Q_1}{\left(\dfrac{Q_2+Q_1}{2}\right)} \div \frac{P_2-P_1}{\left(\dfrac{P_2+P_1}{2}\right)} = \frac{2(Q_2-Q_1)}{Q_2+Q_1} \times \frac{P_2+P}{2(P_2-P_1)} = \frac{(Q_2-Q_1)}{Q_2+Q_1} \times \frac{P_2+P}{(P_2-P_1)}$$

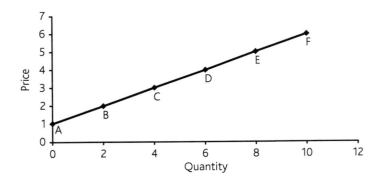

Figure 3.21 *Supply curve*

Feedback

Price of eggs	Supply	Points on curve	Arc elasticity of supply	
1	0	A		
2	20	B	A to B	4.00
3	40	C	B to C	0.44
4	60	D	C to D	0.16
5	80	E	D to E	0.08
6	100	F	E to F	0.05

The theoretical range for elasticity of supply is $0 < |PES| < \infty$

where

PES = 0, this indicates perfect price inelasticity

$0 < |PES| < 1$, price inelasticity

$|PES| = 1$, unit elasticity

$1 < |PES| < \infty$, price elasticity

$|PES| = \infty$, perfectly price elastic.

The diagrams in figure 3.22 show different supply conditions as represented by supply curves of varying degrees of elasticity.

At this point, however, it is important to consider the time period within which the elasticity is considered, due to the fact that the degree of elasticity is dependent on the time period allowed for response. In the short run, it is therefore expected that because the time period allowed for responding tends to be short, the elasticity of supply would tend to be lower than over the long run when the firm is allowed a greater period of flexibility.

There are a number of other factors that influence the price elasticity of supply of a commodity. These include the following:

- The greater the number of firms in an industry, the greater the industry's response to a change in price of a commodity. Thus if the price of a commodity increases then, other things constant, many firms will be able to bring more of this commodity onto the market than one firm.
- If a firm has spare capacity, then it can respond more quickly to changes in price as compared to if it operated at full capacity.
- If a commodity can be easily stored, then its price elasticity of supply will be higher than a commodity that cannot be stored. This is evident as a firm producing a durable good that it stores can run down stocks to meet improvements in price.
- Over time, firms can respond to changes in prices more competently and so the price elasticity of supply will be high.

Activity 3.4
Calculate the elasticity of supply between each of the points on the supply curve in Figure 3.21.

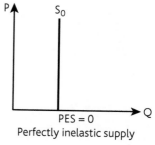
PES = 0
Perfectly inelastic supply

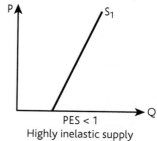
PES < 1
Highly inelastic supply

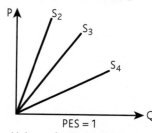
PES = 1
Unitary elastic supply passes through the origin

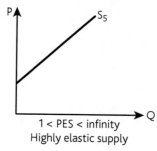
1 < PES < infinity
Highly elastic supply

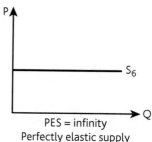
PES = infinity
Perfectly elastic supply

Figure 3.22 *Ranges of elasticity of supply*

Example

Producer surplus

In Figure 3.23 the shaded area represents the producer's surplus. Specifically, producer surplus refers to the benefits obtained by producers by selling a commodity at a given market price. As on the diagram, at a market price of P_1, Q_1 units are sold. Producers benefit from this market price because of the fact that they were willing to accept less than P_1 for all the 0 to $(Q_1 - 1)$ units. Therefore, producer surplus is the area above the supply curve but below the price line.

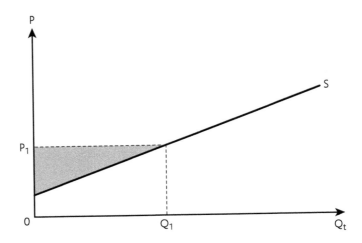

Figure 3.23 *Producer surplus*

Conclusion

In this chapter the four factors of production were identified: land, labour, capital and entrepreneurship. The theory of production was also discussed. The associated short-run and long-run concepts of production were also covered; in particular, the law of diminishing returns was detailed.

The stages of production were also identified. The theory of supply was discussed in this context also. As well as the concept of producer surplus. The chapter closed with a discussion of the concept of elasticity of supply.

Key points

- The production of goods and services requires the utilisation of factors of production. Standard economic literature typically identifies four factors of production, specifically land, labour, capital and entrepreneurial talent.
- Labour is defined as the human contribution to the production of goods and services, and consists of time and energy spent on producing output. It includes the actual physical work as well as the mental activities involved in production.
- The entrepreneur refers to the factor of production that combines all the other factors of production in the productive process.

- Classical economists regard capital as those commodities that are man-made and used in the production of other goods and services.
- Land refers to the resources provided by nature and includes mineral deposits, wind and wave power as well as solar power.
- The theory of production refers to the study of the relationship between factor inputs and output, that is, it is a study of the changes in output when the amounts of factors of production utilised are varied in the production process.
- The production function refers to a technically efficient combination of factor inputs that, when fed into the production process, gives a particular level of output.
- The law of diminishing returns states that as additional amounts of a variable factor are applied to a fixed factor, first the marginal, then the average and finally the total product will fall.
- Costs are a function of the level of inputs employed in the production process.
- Normal average total cost curves (ATC) are U-shaped. The shape of this curve is due primarily to the principles and laws upon which the two components of average cost are based.
- Supply refers to the amount of a commodity that is brought to the market at a particular price over a specific period of time.
- A movement along the supply curve is caused by changes in the commodity's own market price.
- Changes in the non-price factors that affect supply result in a change in supply rather than a change in the quantity supplied. A change in supply is evidenced by a shift of the supply curve, either rightward or leftward.
- Price elasticity of supply measures the responsiveness of quantity supplied to changes in the commodity's own price.

4 Market equilibrium

Content

- The concept of the market
- Equilibrium price and equilibrium quantity
- Use of demand and supply data to calculate equilibrium price and quantity
- Changes in conditions of supply and demand
- The effects of controls on equilibrium:
  - The effects of taxation and subsidies on market equilibrium
  - The incidence of an indirect tax

The concept of the market

In economics the concept of the market relates to any situation where buyers and sellers interact to exchange goods and services. In the most literal sense, marketplaces are places where goods and services are bought and sold. However, in the modern economy, markets have expanded to include virtual interaction such as via the world wide web where millions of buyers and sellers can interact in real time.

Market equilibrium

Market equilibrium analysis draws together the market demand and market supply curves and seeks to identify the market clearing or equilibrium price and output levels on the market.

Table 4.1 *Market equilibrium for crab in a week*

Price of crab	Quantity of crab demanded	Quantity of crab supplied
1	21	3
2	19	5
3	17	7
4	15	15
5	13	18
6	11	22
7	9	26
8	7	31
9	5	39
10	3	47

In the market schedule in Table 4.1 above, the market demand and supply schedules from the previous discussion are brought together. As can be seen, at the price of $4 the quantity demanded of crab is the same as the quantity supplied of crab. This price is unique; at no other price level is the market in equilibrium. More formally, equilibrium occurs at some P_i where $Q^d_n = Q^s_n$.

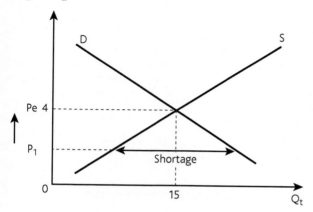

Figure 4.1 *Market equilibrium and shortages*

When market price is below the equilibrium level, the quantity demanded will be greater than the amount supplied. This type of situation refers to a shortage (see Figure 4.1). Prices will tend to increase as consumers begin to offer higher prices for the good. Quantity demanded will begin to fall off and quantity supplied will begin to increase. This action–reaction process will continue up to the point where exactly what is demanded by consumers will be supplied by producers, that is, equilibrium will be restored.

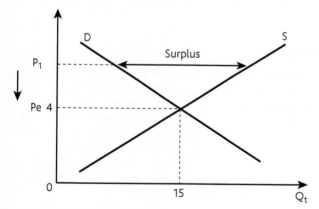

Figure 4.2 *Market equilibrium and surpluses*

When market price is above the equilibrium price, quantity supplied is greater than the quantity demanded. This situation is known as a surplus (see Figure 4.2). Prices would tend to fall as suppliers begin to lower their prices. Consumers would respond by increasing their quantity demanded. This action–reaction process will continue until equilibrium is restored.

Demand and supply: changes in conditions

The equilibrium price that prevails in any one market is maintained as long as the conditions of demand and supply remain the same. This section takes the example of demand for crab to investigate developments in the market that would arise when market demand and/or supply conditions change.

A rise in demand

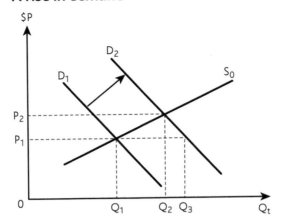

Figure 4.3 *Effects of a rise in demand; outward shift of the demand curve*

Assume initially that the market for crab is in equilibrium with a price level P_1 and quantity traded Q_1 (see Figure 4.3). If there were an increase in demand, then a shortage $(Q_3 - Q_1)$ would develop at the initial price level. The shortage is removed as competition for the available supply bids up the price level, which in turn causes an extension in the quantity of the commodity supplied from Q_1 to Q_2. Equilibrium in the market is re-attained where the new demand curve D_2 meets the supply curve, that is, at price P_2. The increase in demand has increased both the price level and the equilibrium quantity traded of the commodity.

Decrease in demand

If the taste pattern of households were to change away from crab (induced say by a chemical found in crabs that had negative implications for health), then at every price level the household would buy fewer than before. If the initial price level was P_1 (and quantity traded Q_1), then the decrease in demand would result in the emergence of a surplus $(Q_1 - Q_2)$ at the price level P_1 (see Figure 4.4). In such a situation, suppliers, in order to get rid of excess stock, would lower their prices and, as prices decrease, there would be an extension in demand. Prices would settle at P_2 and the equilibrium quantity traded would fall to Q_3.

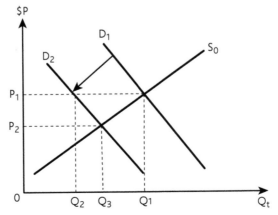

Figure 4.4 *Effects of a decrease in demand on price and quantity traded, leftward shift of the demand curve*

Rise in supply

During the rainy season the number of crabs a supplier can bring to the market is greater at every price level than before simply because the number of crabs available to be caught increases as the rain encourages a break in their hibernation practices. This can also be interpreted as saying that the supply curve shifts rightward. Assume that initially the market was in equilibrium at the price of P_1 with Q_1 crabs traded (see Figure 4.5). An increase in supply means that at the price level P_1, the quantity supplied of crabs is greater than the quantity demanded of crabs and a surplus develops on the market of magnitude $Q_2 - Q_1$. This surplus exerts downwards pressure on prices until a price such as P_2 is attained with Q_3 crabs traded.

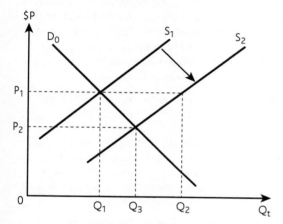

Figure 4.5 *Effects of an increase in supply on price and quantity supplied*

A decrease in supply

During intense periods of dry season, the number of crabs available is limited and the supplier can thus bring only a limited number of crabs into the market. This can alternatively be interpreted as saying that the supply curve of the producer has moved leftwards from S_1 to S_2 as shown in Figure 4.6 below. At the initial price level P_1, there is now a shortage of $Q_1 - Q_2$. Competition among individual buyers would eventually force the price level upwards until a price such as P_2 is reached; the demand for the commodity is once again equal to the supply, the equilibrium quantity traded is now Q_3.

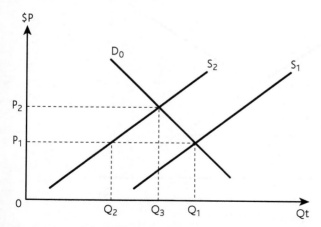

Figure 4.6 *Effects of a decrease in supply on price and quantity supplied*

Table 4.2 *Summary of changes in the conditions of demand and supply on equilibrium price and quantity*

	Price	Quantity
Increase in demand	Increase	Increase
Decrease in demand	Decrease	Decrease
Increase in supply	Decrease	Increase
Decrease in supply	Increase	Decrease

The impact of changes in supply and demand can be summed up in Table 4.2.

The effects of price controls on equilibrium

Price ceiling

A price ceiling represents the maximum price that can be legally charged in an economy for a particular good or service. Price ceilings are often tagged on government houses. For state-provided housing, governments generally charge a maximum price which is very low. This sometimes results in excess demand for government-provided houses.

Another price ceiling that government sometimes imposes is an interest rate ceiling. The rate of interest is treated in the economic literature as the price of capital. Governments sometimes think that if the price of capital falls, that is, if it becomes cheaper to borrow money from the bank, then more investors will borrow funds for investment. This will add to the stock of capital and can lead to economic growth.

If a price ceiling creates a shortage then this may require non-price rationing techniques, where goods and services are allocated to consumers on the basis of willingness to pay. One simple form of non-price rationing is 'first come, first served'. If the price of the good has an opportunity cost or the time spent waiting is excessive and the perceived benefit of the good is thought to be lower than the sum of the price and opportunity costs, then some consumers may go without the good.

With price ceilings and non-price rationing some consumers may be willing to pay more for the commodity than the government legislated price. A black market occurs when the suppliers of a product provide the good to customers that are both willing and able to pay prices above the legislated maximum.

Price ceilings tend to be set below the market equilibrium price, as shown in Figure 4.7. The main aim of the imposition of price ceilings is to allow increased access to a good or service to individuals who would be unable to afford it at the going market price. Price ceilings, however, as illustrated below, tend to result in a shortage on the market.

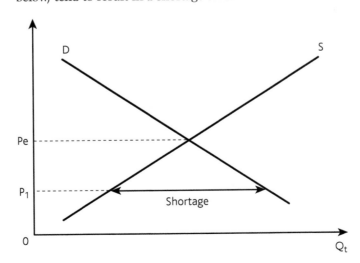

Figure 4.7 *Market equilibrium and price ceiling*

Activity 4.1

1 Consider the following table showing the trends in demand and supply for student apartments around a university campus. Illustrate:

  a the demand curve and the supply curve for apartments

  b the equilibrium price of apartments and the equilibrium quantity.

Price per unit $	Quantity demanded ('00 units per month)	Quantity supplied ('00 units per month)
140	20	39
130	25	34
120	30	30
110	35	25
100	40	22

2 In order to help students the government fixes a price ceiling of $110 per month per room. Show the price ceiling on your diagram.

3 State the likely effect of this policy on the availability of accommodation.

Feedback

1 and 2

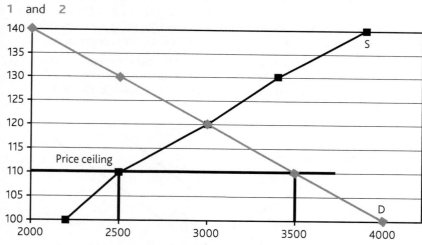

3 This price ceiling would result in a situation of market disequilibrium. The quantity demanded of apartments will be 3,500 while the supply will be 2,500 apartments. There will therefore be a shortage of apartments as demand would outstrip supply.

Price floors

A price floor is a minimum price established by the government below which it is illegal to sell. Price floors are generally set above the market price and act as a safeguard mechanism to ensure a fair return on the good or service. Examples of price floors include set prices for certain agricultural commodities and minimum wage levels for certain types of labour. Minimum wages are typical price floors in developing countries.

Figure 4.8 on page 90 illustrates the market consequences of the imposition of a price floor. Notice that the price floor results in a market situation where the quantity supplied exceeds that of the quantity demanded, that is, a surplus (introduced earlier).

Example

CARICOM: minimum wage

As a regional trading body CARICOM has not evolved to the stage where there is an overall minimum wage throughout the region. In several individual CARICOM countries, however, minimum wage legislation is in place both at a national and industrial level. For example, there is a national minimum wage in Jamaica and Trinidad and Tobago, as well as a minimum wage that is separate and distinct from the national level for certain individual industries, such as the petroleum industry in Trinidad and Tobago and the industrial security guards in Jamaica.

Activity 4.2

Why might a government impose price floors despite their empirically negative effects?

Feedback

A price floor may have negative consequences, but governments implement them to act as a safeguard mechanism to ensure a fair return on the goods and services. For instance, the minimum wage is the most common type of price floor implemented by governments. By doing this they are ensuring that workers are fairly treated by a standardised measure, so that no matter the skill level of the individual, every worker is at least paid a wage that can allow them access to a basic standard of living.

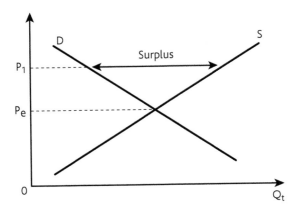

Figure 4.8 *Market equilibrium and price floors*

The effects of taxation and subsidies on market equilibrium

Taxes can be either indirect or direct. Direct taxes are applied to incomes while indirect taxes are applied to goods and services. The analysis will be on indirect taxes since they will affect supply.

Indirect taxes can be either specific or *ad valorem*. A specific tax is a lump sum tax applied to a product. Hence, if wine is being supplied and a specific tax of $5 is applied, even if one bottle of wine is produced or 10,000 bottles, the $5 does not change. A specific tax will cause the price to increase for each level of output and will cause a parallel shift of the supply curve to the left.

The equilibrium price will increase from P_0 to P_1 and the quantity demanded will reduce from Q_0 to Q_1. The full amount of the tax is indicated by the parallel distance between the two supply curves as shown in Figure 4.9.

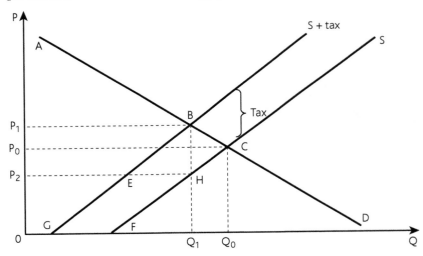

Figure 4.9 *Imposition of a specific tax*

The tax reduces consumer surplus from P_0AC to P_1AB and also reduces producer surplus from $0P_0CF$ to $0P_2EG$. Government revenue earned is represented by the area P_2P_1BH. The deadweight loss is HBC.

The incidence of a tax is the burden that parties bear when a tax is imposed. The consumer bears P_1-P_0 of the tax while the producer bears P_0-P_2 of the tax.

Ad valorem taxes are charged on every unit of the product. Hence if an *ad valorem* tax of 15 per cent is applied, the amount of tax increases as the amount of the product produced and sold increases. If one unit is sold for $1, the amount of tax paid is $0.15. If 10 units are sold, the amount of tax is $1.50. The *ad valorem* tax will therefore cause a non-parallel shift of the supply curve to the left as shown in Figure 4.10 below.

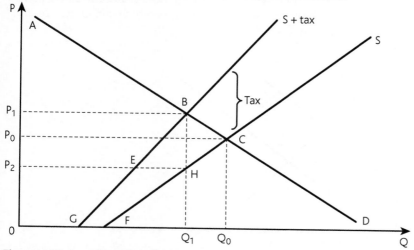

Figure 4.10 *Imposition of an* ad valorem *tax*

The diagrams in Figure 4.11 illustrate the distribution of the incidence of burden of the imposition of a tax between suppliers and consumers.

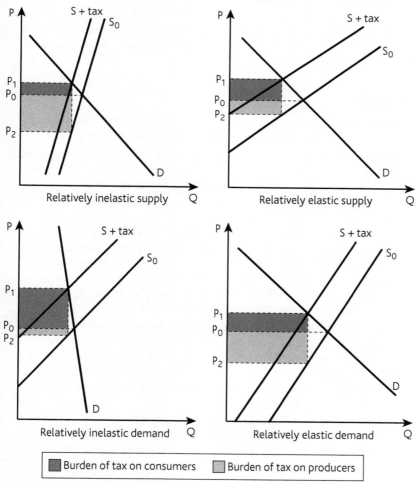

Figure 4.11 *Distribution of the incidence of burden on the imposition of a tax between consumers and producers*

Table 4.3 *Distribution of the incidence of burden of a tax*

Degree of elasticity	Party bearing the greater burden of tax
Inelastic supply	Producers
Elastic supply	Consumers
Inelastic demand	Consumers
Elastic demand	Producers

Table 4.3 summarises the information in the diagrams in Figure 4.11.

Subsidies on production will effectively shift the supply curve rightward until the vertical distance between the original and new supply curves is equal to the per unit subsidy. In Figure 4.12, notice that the entire benefit of the imposition of the subsidy is $P_1 - P_{1-s}$, of which consumers receive $P_1 - P_2$ and producers $P_2 - P_{1-s}$.

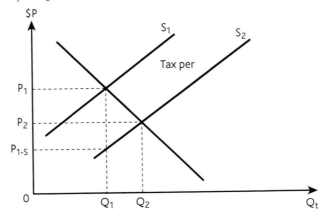

Figure 4.12 *Effects of a production subsidy*

Conclusion

The chapter discusses the concept of market equilibrium and identifies those factors that result in changes in equilibrium price and production levels. The impact of price controls, taxation and subsidies on market equilibrium are also discussed.

Key points

- In economics the concept of the market relates to any situation where buyers and sellers interact to exchange goods and services.
- Market equilibrium analysis draws together the market demand and market supply curves and seeks to identify the market clearing or equilibrium price and output levels on the market.
- When market price is below the equilibrium level, the quantity demanded will be greater than the amount supplied. This type of situation refers to a shortage. Prices will tend to increase as consumers begin to offer higher prices for the good. Quantity demanded will begin to fall off and quantity supplied will begin to increase. This action–reaction process will continue up to the point where exactly what is demanded by consumers will be supplied by producers, that is, equilibrium will be restored.
- When market price is above the equilibrium price, quantity supplied is greater than the quantity demanded. This situation is known as a surplus. Prices would tend to fall as suppliers begin to lower their prices. Consumers would respond by increasing their quantity demanded. This action–reaction process will continue until equilibrium is restored.
- A price ceiling represents the maximum price that can be legally charged in an economy for a particular good or service. A price floor is a minimum price established by the government below which it is illegal to sell.

End test

1   Hannah decides to stay at home to do some work rather than go to the mall. What is the opportunity cost of her decision?

   a   the enjoyment she would have derived from a visit to the mall

   b   the improvement in the mark she would obtain for her assignment

   c   the increase in her travelling expenses

   d   the money she would have spent at the mall

2   The central problem of economics is how to:

   a   distribute income and wealth   c   allocate resources between competing uses

   b   reach full employment   d   resolve the conflict between economics and politics

3   The price mechanism can be described as:

   a   the relationship between factor inputs and output

   b   the arithmetic relationship between demand and supply

   c   the guiding principle of the free-market system, also known as the invisible hand

   d   a geometric relationship between demand and supply

4   Water is relatively cheap, even though it is a necessity. Diamonds, on the other hand, are not a necessity but are relatively more expensive. The key reasoning for this paradox of value is that:

   a   consumers are regarded as irrational beings

   b   because of their scarcity, the marginal utility of diamonds tends to be higher than the marginal utility of water due to its abundance

   c   there is one main diamond producer in the market

   d   there is no discernable relationship between total and marginal utility

5   The rational consumer will allocate their income in such a way to ensure that:

   a   marginal utility obtained from each good consumed is equal

   b   total utility obtained from each good consumed is equal

   c   marginal utility from each good consumed is maximised

   d   total utility from consuming the particular good as a whole is maximised

6   The theory that states that consumers would be in equilibrium when the ratio of marginal utility and price is equalised for each commodity consumed is known as:

   a   equimarginal utility   c   rational consumption law

   b   law of demand and supply   d   equilibrium price and quantity

7   Which of the following statements is false as regards indifference curves:

   a   Indifference curves have negative slopes.

   b   The marginal rate of substitution between good X and good Y increases as more of good X is utilised by the consumer.

   c   The marginal rate of substitution between good X and good Y decreases as more of good X is consumed by the consumer.

   d   An indifference curve that is closer to the origin represents a lower level of utility.

8   A budget line:

   a   has a positive slope

   b   shows how the expenditures of firms change as consumers' income increases

   c   has a gradient that is equal to $- (P_X/P_Y)$

   d   is also called an isoprofit line

9   The position of a budget line would shift away from the origin if:

   a   consumer income decreases   c   the price of one good falls

   b   consumer income increases   d   the price of one good rises

10 A consumer would be in equilibrium when:
   a they can sketch its indifference map
   b they can purchase all their basic necessities and still generate savings
   c $MRS_{X,Y} = P_X/P_Y$
   d two indifference curves intersect

11 The price effect is comprised of the:
   a income and substitution effects
   b income effects
   c substitution effects
   d none of the above

12 The law of variable proportions states that:
   a as more factors of production are utilised output will rise initially and then fall
   b as more factors of production are employed, output will rise but at a diminishing rate
   c as more variable factors of production are added to a fixed factor, output will rise at a faster rate initially and then fall
   d as more variable factors of production are added to a fixed factor, output will rise at a decreasing rate after a certain point

13 What is the difference between diminishing returns to a variable factor and decreasing returns to scale?
   a One is a short-run concept and the other a long-run concept.
   b One uses labour-intensive technology and the other capital-intensive technology.
   c One is skill intensive the other is labour intensive.
   d One requires an abundance of labour and the other capital.

14 MP = AP at which of the follow points?
   a Average product is rising.
   b Marginal product is rising.
   c Average product is at a maximum.
   d Marginal product is at a maximum.

15 APL decreases over the range when:
   a MP_L decreases
   b MP_L increases
   c TP_L decreases
   d $MP_L < AP_L$

16 The profit maximising point of output corresponds to where:
   a marginal cost is equal to marginal revenue
   b demand is equal to supply
   c average revenue is equal to average cost
   d total cost is equal to total revenue

17 In a typical week, Ruth allocates her expenditure amongst three goods: muffins, sweet breads and cakes. The table below shows the price and the related marginal utilities for the goods.

Goods	Muffins	Sweet breads	Cakes
Price ($)	10	4	2
Marginal utility (units)	20	6	4

How should her consumption pattern change so that she maximises utility?

	Muffins	Sweet breads	Cakes
a	Increase	Decrease	Decrease
b	Increase	Decrease	Increase
c	Decrease	Increase	Decrease
d	Decrease	Decrease	Increase

18 Indifference curves are associated with which of the following schools of thought?

    a ordinalist   **c** macroeconomics

    b cardinalist   **d** development theory

19 When there are plans to build a plant, the firm is operating in the:

    a short run   **c** momentary period

    b long run   **d** none of the above

20 If a firm's marginal cost of producing a good is increasing:

    a the firm should reduce its production until marginal cost levels off

    b that is a sign that the marginal physical product of some inputs is falling

    c the firm should increase its production

    d the firm must be operating at a loss

End test feedback

1 a   the enjoyment she would have derived from a visit to the mall

2 c   allocate resources between competing uses

3 c   the guiding principle of the free-market system, also known as the invisible hand

4 b   because of their scarcity, the marginal utility of diamonds tends to be higher than the marginal utility of water due to its abundance

5 a   marginal utility obtained from each good consumed is equal

6 a   equimarginal utility

7 b   The marginal rate of substitution between good X and good Y increases as more of good X is utilised by the consumer.

8 c   has a gradient that is equal to $-(P_X/P_Y)$

9 b   consumer income increases

10 c $MRS_{X,Y} = P_X/P_Y$

11 a   income and substitution effects

12 c   as more variable factors of production are added to a fixed factor, output will rise at a faster rate initially and then fall

13 a   One is a short-run concept and the other a long-run concept.

14 c   Average product is at a maximum.

15 d $MP_L < AP_L$

16 a   marginal cost is equal to marginal revenue

17 c   Muffins: decrease; Sweet breads: increase; Cakes: decrease

18 a   ordinalist

19 b   long run

20 b   that is a sign that the marginal physical product of some inputs is falling

Tutor-marked assignment

1   Market equilibrium refers to the situation where
_____ is equal to _____.

2   In a free market, prices are determined through the interaction of
_____ and _____.

3   Effective demand refers to _____
_____.

4   Supply refers to _____
_____.

5   The relation between price and quantity demanded can be expressed
as a _____, a _____ or a
_____.

6   The relationship between price and quantity demanded is _____
_____.

7   A decrease in demand causes equilibrium price to _____and
equilibrium quantity to _____.

8   A change in income or a change in the price of a substitute good results in a
_____ of the demand curve.

9   When the market price is higher than the equilibrium price a
_____ occurs on the market.

10 When the market price is lower than the equilibrium price a
_____ occurs on the market.

Feedback

1   market demand, market supply
2   demand, supply
3   demand that is backed by the ability to pay
4   the amount of a good that is brought onto the market at a particular
price over a particular period of time, *ceteris paribus*
5   demand function, demand schedule, demand curve
6   negative or inverse
7   decrease, decrease
8   shift
9   surplus
10 shortage

5

Market structure

General objectives

On completion of this module, you should be able to:

appreciate the distinction between the different types of market structures

develop awareness of the causes of market failure

appreciate the measures that can be adopted to reduce or eliminate market failure

appreciate the arguments that suggest that government intervention may not necessarily improve economic performance.

Specific objectives

You should be able to:

outline the goals of the firm

explain how firms measure profits

explain the concepts of average, marginal and total revenue

explain the concept of market structure

outline the characteristics of the different market structures

distinguish between the different market structures

explain the factors that influence the pricing and output decisions of the firm

calculate measures of industrial concentration

interpret measures of industrial concentration.

Content

- Profit maximisation, growth, satisficing, sales and revenue maximisation, market dominance
- Total revenue, total cost, normal and economic (abnormal) profit
- Relationship between average, marginal and total revenue
- Types of market structures: perfect competition, monopoly including price discrimination, monopolistic competition, oligopoly and cartels
- Characteristics of the different market structures:
  - Barriers to entry
  - Control over market and price
  - Nature of the good
  - Numbers of buyers and sellers
  - Competitive behaviour and performance
- Focus on all characteristics of the different markets in addition to profit maximisation
  - Examples of close approximations of market structures in the Caribbean
- Marginal cost and marginal revenue, total cost and total revenue, marginal cost pricing and average cost pricing
- Herfindahl Hirschman Index – the percentage of an industry's output produced by its four largest firms (four-firm concentration ratio):

$$HI = \sum_{i=1}^{n} S_i^2$$

where S_i is the market share of firm i in the market, and n is the number of firms

- Interpretation related to market structures
- Limitations of measures of industrial concentration

Goals of the firm

The standard neo-classical school of economics has proposed that profit maximisation is the single goal of the firm. However, with the emergence of behavioural economics it was shown that firms also pursued other objectives. These behavioural theories sought to identify that the organisation comprised several groups of stakeholders and that the aims of these groups may often differ.

Any corporation can be shown to comprise several groups of stakeholders, including employees, managers, shareholders and customers.

Some of the varying objectives that a firm can pursue besides profit maximisation include:

- Satisficing: this refers to the practice of setting the minimum acceptable level of achievement. Firms may aim to achieve only satisfactory rather than maximum results. The practice of satisficing is aiming to obtain results that are good enough. It refers to the decision-making strategy towards adequacy rather than optimality.

- Sales revenue maximisation: this objective was first proposed by Baumol in 1959. Baumol's research indicated that in corporations that are controlled by managers (rather than owners or shareholders), annual salaries and other perks were closely related to total sales revenue rather than profits. As such, managers tended to focus on maximising sales revenue.
- Limit pricing: predatory pricing may be practised by firms that are trying to gain market share or maintain a monopoly position in the market. Limit pricing involves lowering prices to essentially force competitors to operate at a loss.

Market structure

There are several types of market structures that exist today. Market structures refer to the conditions under which a product or service is bought and sold. In this case, therefore, it is reasonable to suggest that because the market conditions under which crude oil or natural gas is traded are different from those under which cement is traded, for example, then the structure of the oil market is different from that of the 'doubles' market. Market structures are therefore distinguished on the basis of their characteristics.

There are four main market types that are covered by this chapter; these are perfect competition, monopoly, monopolistic competition and oligopoly. Each of the market types occur along a spectrum as shown in Figure 5.1, with perfect competition and pure monopoly occurring at either ends, and each of the other market types characterised by tendencies towards either perfect competition or monopoly.

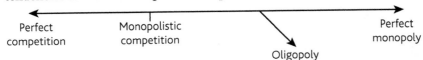

Figure 5.1 *Various market structures*

At this point it should be noted that pure monopoly and pure perfect competition situations are hypothetical. In reality these extremes do not exist, just varying degrees of either. The characteristics of each structure are discussed below as well as the short- and long-run conditions that prevail under each market structure.

Perfect competition

The theory of perfect competition is discussed in the following manner. The assumptions or the characteristics on which the market is premised will be given, after which the demand and supply functions for the firm will be discussed followed by the possible short- and long-run positions of the firm and the industry. The firm refers to a single entity or producer that engages in the production of a specific commodity or service. An industry refers to a group of firms that produce identical goods and/or services.

Perfect competition refers to a market structure that is characterised by the absence of rivalry. In its purest sense, the term 'rivalry' is associated with competition and as such firms in this market structure do not compete against each other for market share or customer loyalty as in other market structures. The other characteristic assumptions of perfect competition are detailed in the section below.

Assumptions of perfect competition

The theory of perfect competition is characterised by several assumptions. These include:

1 The government does not interfere with the operation of the market. Its main role is to provide an infrastructural and institutional base within which the market operates. This includes a national police service, a national army and a bureau of standards. The bureau of standards is a government-mandated organisation with the responsibility of ensuring that consumers are not exploited by business organisations.

2 There are large numbers of buyers and sellers in the market. The implication of this is that no one buyer or seller has control over market prices, that is, no one producer or consumer can influence the market price of the commodity by either changing supply or demand levels respectively.

3 The market is characterised by the freedom of entry and exit of firms. There are no barriers to entry and resources can move easily into the industry without any limitations. The implication of this characteristic is that in the long run all firms in the industry will earn only normal profits. This will be dealt with in detail later in this chapter.

4 The perfectly competitive firm operates in an industry where each firm produces the same commodity, that is, the market is characterised by product homogeneity. This assumption together with assumption 2 implies that the individual firm is a 'price taker' and, as a result, its demand curve is perfectly elastic at the going market price.

5 All economic agents participating in the perfectly competitive market (consumers and producers) are assumed to have perfect knowledge. This assumption ensures that both consumers and producers are informed of all market conditions when making decisions. Perfect knowledge helps to ensure that scarce resources are optimally allocated.

Demand curve of the firm

For simplicity, let us assume that the price of a can of cola does not change regardless of the amount that the market demands. Assuming that a can of cola costs $1, then selling two cans will earn the shopkeeper revenues of $2, and so on.

By deduction,

$$\text{TR}_2 \text{ (total revenue from 2 cans of cola sold)} = \$2$$

$$\text{TR}_1 \text{ (total revenue from 1 can of cola sold)} = \$1$$

As with costs and production, a firm's revenue can also be discussed in aggregate (e.g. total revenue) or per unit (e.g. average revenue and marginal revenue). The average revenue (AR) and the marginal revenue (MR) of the firm is calculated as:

$$\text{AR}_2 = \frac{\text{TR}_2}{2} = \frac{\$2}{2} = \$1 = \text{P}$$

$$\text{MR}_2 = \text{TR}_2 - \text{TR}_1 = \$2 - \$1 = \$1 = \text{P}$$

Thus, in an environment where the price of the commodity does not change, the firm's average revenue is the same as its price and marginal revenue. So we can write P = MR = AR. Assume that demand is exogenously determined, meaning that it is determined by the sum total of the interaction of all producers and all consumers in the market and not just one economic agent; at the market price level of $P per unit, consumers can buy any number of units of the output from the perfectly competitive firm. For a perfectly competitive firm, the demand curve is horizontal or perfectly elastic (see Figure 5.2).

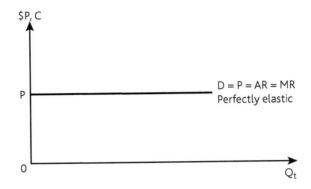

Figure 5.2 *Relationship between P, AR and MR in perfect competition*

Determination of the firm's supply curve

To derive the firm's supply curve in the short run, we can proceed as follows. At the price P_3, the firm will supply Q_3 units of output. Suppose now that the price level falls to P_1. At the price P_1, the firm's average revenue is less than its average total costs per unit of output but greater than its average variable costs, that is, AR > AVC. The advice to the firm would be to continue to produce in the short run as it can cover its operational costs and still make something extra to reduce the magnitude of losses on its fixed costs.

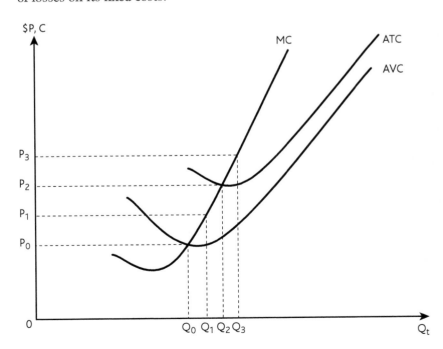

Figure 5.3 *Derivation of the short-run supply curve of a firm in perfect competition*

At a price such as P_0, however, the firm will still produce but, for any price level for which the market price is lower than the average variable cost, the firm will not produce, simply because it would not be able to cover even its operational cost.

The lowest point on the average variable cost curve is called the shutdown point of a firm in the short run, the lowest market price for which the firm will remain in operation. If the market price falls below this level, then the firm will cease production immediately.

The supply curve is derived from the upward sloping portion of the MC curve above the minimum point of the average variable cost curve, as shown in Figure 5.4.

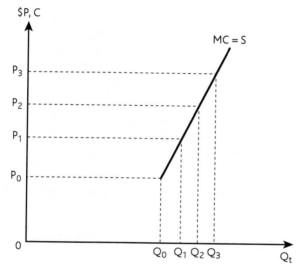

Figure 5.4 *The short-run supply curve of a firm in perfect competition*

Equilibrium of the firm

The perfectly competitive firm (and so too firms in other market structures) is in equilibrium when it maximises its profits (π), which is defined as the difference between total cost and total revenues, that is,

$$\pi = TR - TC$$

This equilibrium can be shown using two approaches: the total approach or the marginal approach.

The total approach

This method compares the total revenue a firm receives from producing a particular level of output with the associated total cost to obtain the largest positive difference. The output level that corresponds to this largest level is the profit maximising output. An alternative way of looking at this situation is as a loss-minimising option. Firms may be incurring losses in the short run. However losses in the short run do not imply that the firm should close down. As a matter of fact, because of the cost structure of the firm, i.e. incurring both fixed and variable costs, the firm may actually be incurring fewer losses by remaining in operation, in which case the optimal level of output is associated with the lowest level of losses.

Figure 5.5 on page 102 shows the total revenue and total cost curves of the firm. The total revenue curve is a straight line through the origin, indicating that the price is constant at all levels of output. The slope of the TR curve is equal to the MR of the firm. The total cost curve of the firm has an elongated inverted 'S' shape. In the early stages of production, as marginal and average total costs fall, the TC increases at a slower rate, but as marginal costs increase, due to the law of diminishing returns, costs increase at a faster pace.

At the level of output Q_0 and Q_2 the firm is breaking even as its total revenue and total cost are identical. At Q_1, however, where the vertical distance between the TC and TR curve is greatest, the firm is making the maximum amount of profit possible. The firm therefore maximises its profit at the output level Q_1 where the distance between the TR and TC curves is the greatest.

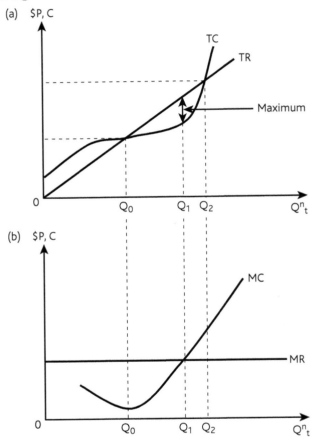

Figure 5.5 *Profit maximisation using the total cost and total revenue approach*

Marginal approach

The marginal approach is the more widely used method of determining the profit-maximising point of operation for a firm, in that it compares the changes or additions to profitability as a result of producing and selling one more unit of the commodity.

This approach uses the concepts of marginal cost and marginal revenue to determine the changes in profitability, where marginal profitability refers to the difference between marginal revenue and marginal cost.

Consider the marginal cost and marginal revenue curve illustrated in Figure 5.5 above. At a level of production such as Q_0 the firm can earn a higher profit by increasing the level of output. This occurs due to the fact that marginal revenue is greater than marginal cost, in which case marginal profitability will be positive. Total profit expands only until the Q_{1st} unit of the commodity is produced and sold. Thus the firm will not cease production at Q_0 but will increase output until Q_1. If the firm increases production beyond Q_1 units of output, each additional unit produced will incur a loss as the marginal cost of production will outstrip the marginal revenue the firm obtains from its sale.

The marginal approach to profit maximisation can therefore be summarised as:

If MC < MR, the total profit has not been maximised and it makes sense for the firm to expand output.

If MC > MR the firm's profit is falling, then it makes sense for the firm to cut its production.

The conclusion therefore is that:

If MC = MR, and that the firm's marginal cost curve cuts the marginal revenue curve from below, short-run profits are maximised. In Figure 5.6 below, profits are maximised where marginal cost is equal to marginal revenue. This corresponds to output level Q.

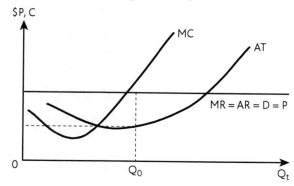

Figure 5.6 *Profit maximisation*

Activity 5.1

Consider the numerical example below. Plot these curves to determine the profit-maximising level of output.

	P$	TR	AR	MR	TC	TVC	TFC	ATC	AFC	AVC	MC
1	10	10	10		13	8	5	13.00	5.00	8.00	
2	10	20	10	10	19	14	5	9.50	2.50	7.00	6
3	10	30	10	10	23	18	5	7.67	1.67	6.00	4
4	10	40	10	10	28	23	5	7.00	1.25	5.75	5
5	10	50	10	10	34	29	5	6.80	1.00	5.80	6
6	10	60	10	10	41	36	5	6.83	0.83	6.00	7
7	10	70	10	10	51	46	5	7.29	0.71	6.57	10
8	10	80	10	10	64	59	5	8.00	0.63	7.38	13
9	10	90	10	10	78	73	5	8.67	0.56	8.11	14
10	10	100	10	10	94	89	5	9.40	0.50	8.90	16
11	10	110	10	10	112	107	5	10.18	0.45	9.73	18

Feedback

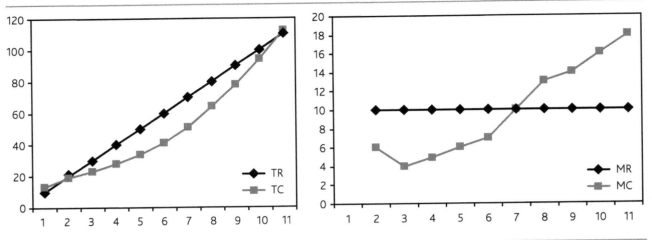

Normal and abnormal profit and profit maximisation

Built into the cost curve of firms is a minimum amount of profit that is necessary to keep the factors of production in their current position of employment. When a firm is breaking even in economics we say that such a firm is making only normal profits. Normal profits occur when TR = TC for a particular level of output, that is, where AR = ATC.

Abnormal profits occur where AR > ATC. Abnormal profits refer to a situation in which AR > ATC, or TR > TC of production.

Profit maximisation is the overarching objective of all firms in business. The profits of a firm are realised by determining the profit per unit, multiplied by the quantity produced and sold, that is:

$$(AR - ATC)Q = \pi$$

Short-run positions of the perfectly competitive firm

Consider Figure 5.7. In (a) interaction of the demand and supply curves for the commodity at the industry level gives an equilibrium price such as

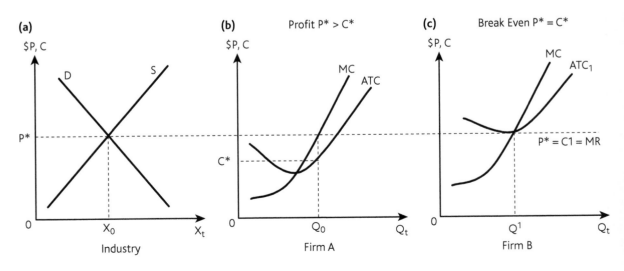

Figure 5.7 *Short run equilibrium of the industry and the firm in perfect competition*

P* and an equilibrium amount of goods X_0 to be traded. This price level P* is the price at which all the existing firms in the market must now sell. In the case illustrated, Firm A (Figure 5.7(b)) will produce Q_0 units of the commodity at a per unit cost of C* with a profit per unit of P* − C*. In this case the particular Firm A is making abnormal profits.

In the case of firms with higher average total costs, such as Firm B (Figure 5.7(c)), then the firm will operate at break even with P* = C_1.

In the short run the firm can also make losses. These losses can adopt three principal permutations; these are non-immediate shutdown losses, on the margin of shutdown and immediate shutdown losses.

With non-immediate shutdown losses, the firm has an average total cost curve such as ATC_3, which is above the average revenue line (see Figure 5.8(a)). At the same time though, the average revenues of the firm cover average variable costs. In equilibrium this perfectly competitive firm will produce a level of output Q* at an average total cost per unit of C_3 and an average variable cost of production AVC_3. Clearly, this firm will be able to cover its variable costs of production but not its total costs. This firm will stay in business in the short run and put the block of resources $(C_3 − P*)Q*$ towards reducing its losses on the total fixed costs.

In another permutation (Figure 5.8(b)), the firm can operate with costs curves such as ATC_4, AVC_4 and MC_4. With these cost curves, the firm is on the margin of leaving the industry immediately. A firm in this position receives marginal and average revenue equal to its average variable cost, indicating that the firm is not making anything more than its variable cost of production. This firm is therefore making losses equal to its total fixed costs. Because the firm is only just able to purchase its variable factor inputs, it will be on the border of leaving the industry. In (b), therefore, it can be said that the firm is producing that level of output Q**, which corresponds to its shutdown point.

In Figure 5.8(c), the firm is making losses and will shut down immediately. Specifically the firm cannot even recover its variable costs of production and so by virtue of producing it is making an ever-increasing loss. This firm will therefore leave the industry immediately and profit-maximise by only making a loss equivalent to its fixed costs.

Perfectly competitive firms in the long run

In the long run, given the assumptions of freedom of entry and exit and the existence of perfect knowledge, firms will enter the industry as they are encouraged by the potential of profits in the short run, while firms will leave the industry if losses are being incurred.

Assuming, for example, that the industry is a net profit-making industry, at the price level P_1 the industry produces X_1 units of X. The presence of profits will act as a signal for resources to flow into the industry. This will lead to a rightward shift of the supply curve for the industry which will result in a fall in price of the commodity X. The price of X will continue to fall until there is no further incentive for resources to flow into this industry. This will only happen when firms in the industry are making only normal profits. At the level of the industry, the fall in the price level over the long run will require that firms change the very size of their plants. In the long run, all firms will have to switch to plants with average total costs curves such as SAC_2 where firms are breaking even.

The long-run equilibrium of the firm will occur when it has altered its plant capacity in order to produce at the minimum point of the long-run average total cost curve (LRATC). The LRATC curve is tangential to the

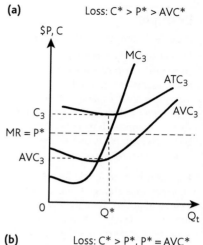

(a) Loss: C* > P* > AVC*

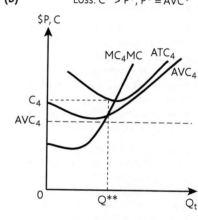

(b) Loss: C* > P*, P* = AVC*

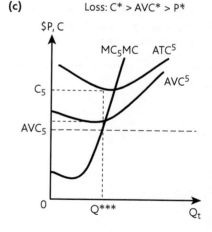

(c) Loss: C* > AVC* > P*

Figure 5.8 *A loss in perfect competition*

Example

Is perfect competition possible?

In reality, purely perfectly competitive markets are a theoretical ideal, against which markets and industries are compared. Several individual markets in the agricultural sector do approach this ideal where one such example is that of the international milk market.

For many international players in this market, although there is some degree of government involvement at the local level, there are some aspects that mirror the theoretical pillars of perfect competition.

For example, the small individual farmer usually has no significant control over the international market price for the commodity. In addition, the product itself is uniformed or homogeneous, because of the extent of regulations imposed on farmers and farming conditions.

For many of the agricultural commodities traded internationally, the market characteristics mirror the premises of perfect competition to a great extent. However, it should be noted that due to the extent of imperfection that characterises trade and industry on the whole, perfect competition in its purest state does not exist.

demand curve (defined by the market price), at the former's lowest point as shown in Figure 5.9. In the long-run scenario, therefore, all firms will be earning only normal profits.

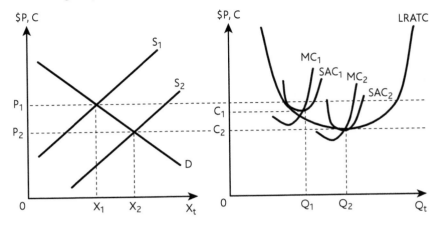

Figure 5.9 *Long-run dynamics in perfect competition*

To summarise, in the long run:

$$P_2 = C_2 = MC_2 = SAC_2 = LAC$$

Monopoly

A monopoly is a market structure that is characterised by only one seller who produces a commodity (or service) for which there are no close substitutes.

Reasons for the existence of a monopoly

There are a number of reasons why monopolies can occur, and these include the following:

- Secret formula: some companies like Angostura Ltd of Trinidad and Tobago produce a commodity that they sell under monopoly conditions. Their market strength resides in the fact that they have a secret formula that no other competitor or potentially competitive firm has been able to breach.

  In some cases the formula may not be secret, but a firm can get monopoly status if it produces a commodity for which it develops a formula and subsequently patents it. One classic example is that of Kentucky Fried Chicken, which boasts a special blend of herbs and spices, the recipe for which is patented.

- By having access to strategic raw materials a firm might be able to have monopoly coverage over the output of some commodities, for example De Beers from South Africa have a near monopoly status because they control a substantial share of the world's diamond supply.

- A monopoly firm can exist because the size of the market allows only one firm to subsist. Monopolies of this type are referred to as natural monopolies. Good examples of these types of monopolies are the public utilities that exist in most CARICOM economies.

- Sometimes an industry may have more than one firm at some point. However, what sometimes occurs is that the most efficient of these firms with the largest resource base can charge lower prices for its commodity than its rivals. Through this type of limit-pricing strategy the more efficient firm can out-compete its rivals and eventually gain control of the market. Another factor that can lead to the creation of a monopoly is that established firms in an industry can build on their goodwill and established credit ratings to obtain preferential access to credit from the existing financial intermediaries. Such firms can use this as a basis for driving other firms out of the market.

- A monopoly can also emerge because the government has offered permission to franchise. One such example is Peter Elias in Trinidad and Tobago, who now holds the franchise for the Miss World Pageant and various other international and regional competitions. This franchise was originally held by the Caribbean Communications Network, however. Another prominent example is that of Prestige Holdings Ltd, the company that holds the Kentucky Fried Chicken franchise in Trinidad and Tobago.

Assumptions of the monopoly

The theory of monopoly is founded upon a number of assumptions. These are as follows:

- The government does not intervene in the workings of the market except if the monopolist contravenes the laws of the land.
- In the monopoly market, there is only one seller and a large number of buyers. The implication of this is that the monopolist has significant control over the market price of the commodity it sells. Monopolists are known as 'price makers'.
- A monopoly has strong market barriers and these barriers are strong enough to ensure that there is no market penetration so that a monopolist's short-run position can extend into the long run.
- The product of the monopolist is unique and has no substitutes.
- The monopoly market structure is characterised by imperfect knowledge and as such sometimes price discrimination occurs. Price discrimination refers to the outright exploitation of market imperfections that allows the monopolist to extract, in some cases, the total consumer surplus.

The demand curve of the monopolist

The demand curve facing the monopolist is the same demand curve facing the industry. This demand curve is downward sloping, as shown in Figure 5.10. The shape of the demand curve has implications for the

Example

Angostura: monopoly producer of bitters

Angostura Bitters was developed by Dr Johann Siegert in 1824. He originally intended the mixture of herbs as a remedy for fever and stomach disorders experienced by soldiers in Venezuela engaged in a war against the Spanish. Due, however, to the political unrest, Siegert's sons Carlos and Alfredo, who had inherited the business after the death of their father, migrated to Trinidad. The rest, as they say, is history, with the company prospering in its new home and surviving bids from international investors from the United States and Canada – both were unsuccessful. Over time the company developed and expanded and remained successful, even diversifying into rum distilling in the mid 1900s. Today the company's products are world renowned and internationally credited.

Angostura Ltd was the recipient of the coveted National Award, the Humming Bird Gold Medal for its contribution to industry in Trinidad and Tobago in 1985.

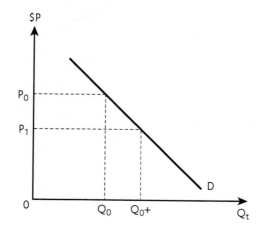

Figure 5.10 *Demand curve of a monopolist*

revenues of the firm. Specifically, if a firm with a downward-sloping demand wants to sell more of its commodity, it has to lower the market price of the commodity.

With a downward-sloping demand curve, the marginal revenue curve of the firm diverges from the average revenue curve. The marginal revenue curve slopes below the average revenue or demand curve, at twice the latter's rate.

Feedback

Activity 5.2

Use the information in Figure 5.10 on page 107 to derive the marginal revenue earned by selling the Q + 1st unit.

In Figure 5.10 on page 107, let the demand curve of the monopolist be such that it sells Q_0 at the price P_0 and $Q_0 + 1$ at the price P_1, that is, to increase output from Q_0 to $Q_0 + 1$, the monopolist has to allow price to fall from P_0 to P_1.

Note that:

$$P_0 Q_0 = TR_0$$
$$P_1 (Q_0 + 1) = TR_1$$
$$TR_1 - TR_0 = MR_1$$
$$MR_1 = P_1 (Q_0 + 1) - P_0 Q_0$$
$$= P_1 Q_0 + P_1 - P_0 Q_0$$
$$= Q_0 (P_1 - P_0) + P_1$$
$$= P_1 + Q_0 (P_1 - P_0)$$
$$= P_1 + Q_0 \text{ (a } -\text{ve amount)}$$
$$= P_1 + \text{(a } -\text{ve amount)}$$
$$\therefore MR_1 < AR_1 = P_1$$
$$\text{But } P_1 = AR_1$$
$$\text{Thus } MR_1 < AR_1$$

The MR curve is therefore lower than the AR curve (Figure 5.11).

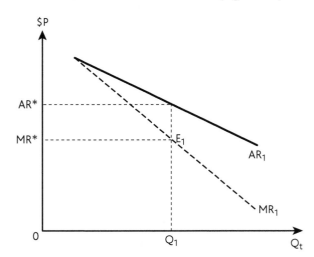

Figure 5.11 *MR and AR curve of a monopolist*

Shape of the monopolist total revenue curve

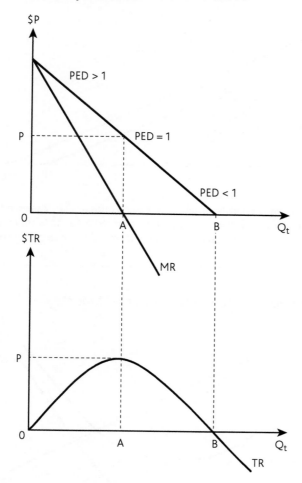

Figure 5.12 *Elasticity and total revenue conditions for a monopolist*

Figure 5.12 shows that where over the range elasticity is greater than unity, or where marginal revenue is positive, increases in quantity will result in an increase in total revenue. However, where demand is price inelastic or where marginal revenue is negative, increases in quantity will result in a reduction in total revenue. Where elasticity is equal to unity or where marginal revenue is zero, total revenue is at its highest. The monopolist should therefore operate along the elastic portion of the demand curve.

Example

Theory application: no monopoly supply curve

The monopolist does not have a supply curve. This happens because there is more than one price for each level of output. Consider the diagram on the following page.

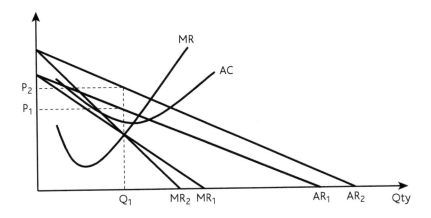

The firm is in equilibrium at output level Q_1 and price level P_1. Assuming now that the demand for the product increases, this shifts the AR and MR curves to AR_2 and MR_2 respectively. The equilibrium quantity remains the same but the price increases to P_2.

Short-run equilibrium of the firm and industry

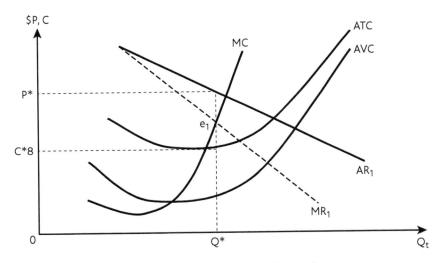

Figure 5.13 *Short-run equilibrium of a monopolist making profits*

As mentioned previously, regardless of the market structure under discussion the firm is in equilibrium at the point where MR = MC. In Figure 5.13 the firm will profit maximise at a point such as e_1 where MR = MC and the MC cuts the MR curve from below. At the profit-maximising point of operation the monopolist will produce Q^* units of output in the short run, which it will sell at P^* dollars per unit. The average cost per unit of this level of output is $\$C^*$ and the profit per unit of the firm is $P^* - C^*$ so that the firm makes a total profit of $(P^* - C^*)Q^*$.

The monopolist's short-run and long-run position are very often identical. This occurs because of the existence of strong barriers to entry and imperfect knowledge. However, the monopolist must be ever wary of potential competition. Potential competition is the threat of competition that can emerge when an industry appears to be generating a very large profit margin.

It is, however, also probable that a monopolist can operate under other conditions such as breaking even or making losses. Figure 5.14 shows that the profit-maximising point of operation is such that it results in average costs and average revenues being equal, indicating that the firm is just breaking even or making only normal profits.

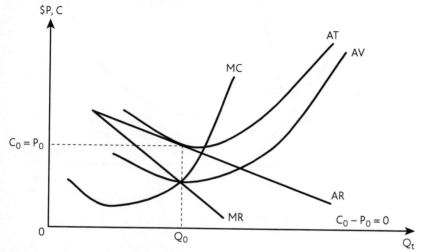

Figure 5.14 *Break even for a monopolist*

A monopolist can also make non-immediate shutdown losses, as illustrated in Figure 5.15. Specifically, with the MR curve and MC curve as outlined, the profit-maximising point of operation coincides with an output level Q_0 and an average cost of production of C_0 and a price level of P_0. With this level of output the loss per unit is $C_0 - P_0$, with total losses given by $Q_0(C_0 - P_0)$.

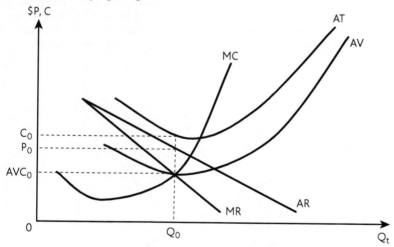

Figure 5.15 *A monopolist making losses*

The long-run position of the monopolist

In the long run the monopolist produces at a scale of output indicated by SAC_0, with an average cost per unit of C_0. However, as indicated in Figure 5.16 on page 112, C_0 is not the lowest possible short-run average cost, nor is the scale of operations the most optimal. Monopolists operate along the falling portion of the long-run average cost curve, or to the left of its minimum point.

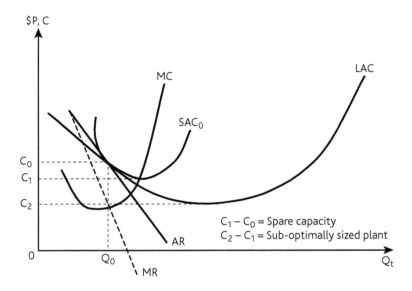

Figure 5.16 *Productive inefficiency in monopoly*

The long-run equilibrium of the monopolist, therefore, is one that reflects excess or spare capacity and this, in turn, implies that the monopolist can lower per unit average costs by increasing output.

Other possible output positions for monopolists

Socially optimal output

The monopolist may produce the output level that corresponds to the point where marginal cost is equal to average revenue or price as shown in Figure 5.17. This point, according to the literature, is the point of allocative efficiency, in that consumers pay what the commodity costs to produce. This level of output exceeds that associated with the point of maximum profitability where marginal cost equals marginal revenue.

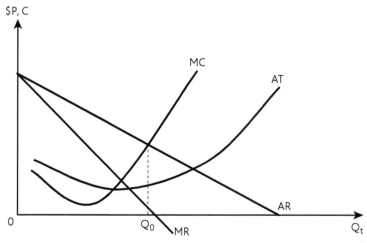

Figure 5.17 *A monopolist producing a socially optimum level of output*

Optimum output

The monopolist may also produce at the point where MC = AC, as shown in Figure 5.18 on page 113. This point is known as productive efficiency. This point also corresponds to a higher level of output, Q_0 in

Figure 5.18, than that which would have been produced under profit-maximisation conditions.

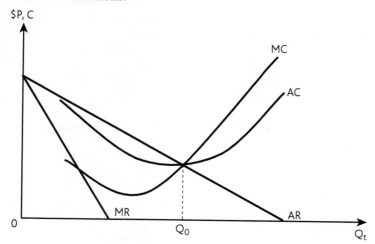

Figure 5.18 *A monopolist producing the optimum level of output*

Price discrimination

Price discrimination refers to a situation in which the same commodity is sold to different consumers in different markets for different prices for reasons not associated with costs. There are two specific preconditions for price discrimination to take place:

- Markets must be separable, with different price elasticities of demand.
- Arbitrage must not be possible.

First-degree price discrimination

With first-degree price discrimination, the seller is able to charge each consumer the maximum amount they are willing to pay for each unit of the commodity purchased. In this case, the producer extracts the entire consumer surplus that would have existed for the consumer. A classic example of this type of discrimination is the case of a visit to a private doctor, where the doctor charges the patient based on the patient's perceived willingness and ability to pay. In its purest form, first-degree price discrimination is called perfect discrimination. Perfect price discrimination is hinged on businesses having perfect knowledge about their customers and using that information to exact the highest payment possible.

Second-degree price discrimination

Second-degree price discrimination is also called quantity discrimination. This occurs where perfect knowledge about customers is not available to firms. This type of discrimination, however, is premised on rational consumer behaviour in willingness to pay for increasing amounts of the commodity, that is, the rational consumer is more willing to pay a higher price for the first unit of the commodity than they are to pay for the fourth unit. This type of rationale is embedded in the downward slope of the demand curve itself.

Second-degree price discrimination therefore occurs where consumers are charged different prices depending on the quantity of the commodity purchased. However, it should be noted that the price differentials at different quantity levels must not be as a result of differing levels of cost.

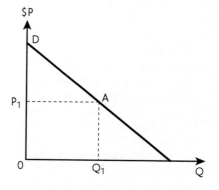

Figure 5.19 *First-degree price discrimination*

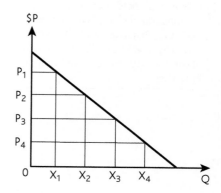

Figure 5.20 *Second-degree price discrimination*

Third-degree price discrimination

Third-degree price discrimination is the most common type of price discrimination, where distinct prices are charged in each of the different markets served. The monopolist can price discriminate only if the nature of the demand elasticities can be effectively identified and exploited. The monopolist will therefore be able to charge a higher price in the market for which the demand for the product is more inelastic, that is, in Market 1 as compared to Market 2, as shown in Figure 5.21.

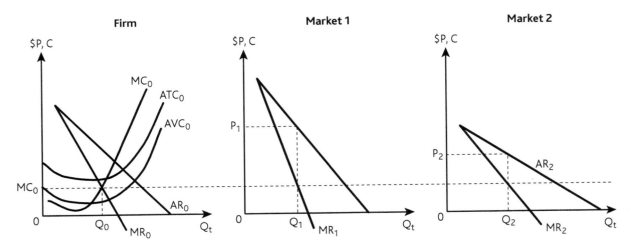

Figure 5.21 *Third-degree price discrimination*

Example

Monopolies in the Caribbean

Lake Asphalt of Trinidad and Tobago (1978) Ltd is a state enterprise that is involved in the mining, processing and export of asphalt products from Trinidad. Lake Asphalt mines asphalt from the Pitch Lake in La Brea and processes it into Cationic Bitumen, a premium-quality enhancer used to pave roadways, highways, bridges and tracks.

Lake Asphalt holds over 20 patents, the most significant of which is the patent for Pelletised Asphalt. This company operates under the purview of the Ministry of Energy and Energy Industries.

Example

Market imperfections associated with Caribbean markets: barriers to entry

Barriers of entry specific to the region include the sheer size of the market. The size of the market in any one Caribbean country and, by extension, the Caribbean as a whole, is generally facilitating to only one firm, in which case the firm is known as a natural monopoly. Other barriers to entry include start-up costs, especially in industries that are considerably capital intensive, such as those existing in the petrochemical industry in Trinidad and Tobago.

Another barrier to entry includes the unavailability of certain types of resources, for example some types of technical labour skills must be imported for certain projects. The unavailability of certain types of labour in the region presents a serious barrier to entry for firms desiring to enter a particular field.

Monopolistic competition

Assumptions of monopolistic competition

The theory of monopolistic competition is founded on the following set of assumptions. The basic assumptions of the model are essentially the same as those of perfect competition, with the exception of the existence of a slightly differentiated product.

▪ The government does not intervene in business except if one of the monopolistically competitive firms infringes on the laws of the land.

▪ A large number of buyers and sellers operate in this market structure. However, the number of sellers is not as large as in perfect competition. The implications of these are such that each of the individual firms controls only a small portion of the market. In this type of environment, collusion is difficult because of the large number of suppliers. In a monopolistically competitive market each of the individual firms acts independent of each other with regards to pricing and output policies.

- This market structure is characterised by weak barriers to entry.
- The firms in this market structure produce a slightly differentiated commodity and hence we do not refer to the firms in a monopolistically competitive industry but rather to the firms in a monopolistically competitive product group.
- Knowledge of the market conditions is assumed to be easily available, that is, perfect knowledge exists.

The 'industry' and 'product group'

The concept of product differentiation creates difficulties in analysing the industry. Differentiated products cannot be summated to create and represent market demand and supply as in the case of homogeneous products; however, the term 'product group' is used to encompass products that are 'closely related' and are close substitutes. The demand for each single product in the group is highly elastic. As such, products included in the group have a high price and cross-elasticities of demand.

Product differentiation

Product differentiation is done to discern one producer's product from those of the other producers in the industry. Product differentiation can be premised on real attributes when the inherent characteristics of the product are different. It can also be fancied, in the case where the products are in essence the same but consumers are persuaded that the products are different through advertising.

The goal of product differentiation is to create a product that is unique in the consumer's mind. Through this, the producer can exercise greater discretion in determining the price. A firm under this market structure is not a price taker but possesses some degree of monopoly power. The extent, however, depends on the firm's success at product differentiation. Thus, there are characteristics of both monopoly and perfect competition in this market structure.

Demand curve in monopolistic competition

Consider Figure 5.22 which highlights the relationship between the demand curves of the various market structures. Observe that, in general,

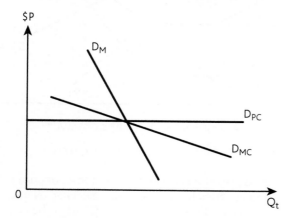

Figure 5.22 *Generalised comparison of the relationship amongst demand curves in monopoly (M), perfect competition (PC) and monopolistic competition (MC)*

Example

Joan Violet Robinson (1903–80)

Joan Violet Robinson, a prominent economist, became famous through her contributions to economic literature in the realm of imperfect competition. In addition, she made significant theoretical inroads in Neo Classical, Neo Ricardian and Post Keynesian economics.

Miss Robinson's first major publication was entitled *The Economics of Imperfect Competition*. In this she discussed a model of competition which was empirically proven to exist between firms, each of which had some monopoly power. In collaboration with an American economist, Edward H. Chamberlin, who had published his *Theory of Monopolistic Competition* mere months prior to her publication, Robinson initiated what was known as the monopolistic competition revolution. This revolution sparked the interests of many economists who believed that most industries or markets are neither perfectly competitive nor completely monopolistic.

Miss Robinson eventually joined the ranks of lecturers at the Cambridge University and published at least three textbooks and numerous articles on issues ranging from accumulation of capital to general equilibrium theory.

Some of her main works include *A Parable of Savings and Investment* (1933), *The Pure Theory of International Trade* (1946) and *The Poverty of Nations* (1968).

the monopolistically competitive firm has a demand curve that is more price elastic than that of a comparable monopoly firm.

Advertising expenditures in monopolistic competition

The influence of advertising is to shift the average variable cost curve of the firm upwards (see Figure 5.23). Thus the average variable cost of the firm is the sum of AVC_p (AVC level of the firm from production alone) and AVC_a (the average variable cost of advertising).

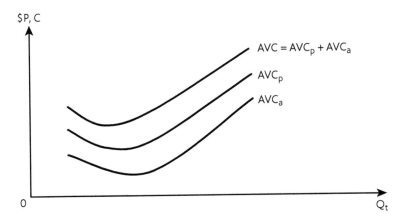

Figure 5.23 *The influence of advertising expenditure on costs*

Short-run equilibrium of the monopolistically competitive firm

In the short run, a typical firm in monopolistic competition can either make profits, normal profits or losses, as illustrated in Figures 5.24, 5.25 and 5.26. Observe that the short-run monopolistically competitive firm is identical to that of a monopolist.

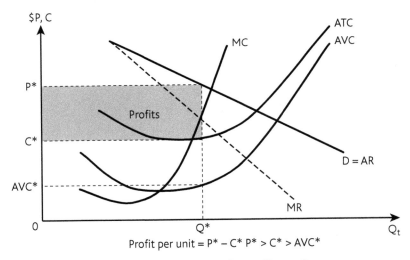

Figure 5.24 *A monopolistically competitive firm making profits*

In Figure 5.24, profit maximisation occurs at a level of output Q with a corresponding average price level P* and an associated average cost per unit of C*. The firm's profit per unit is P* − C* with the total profits of the firm being (P* − C*)Q.

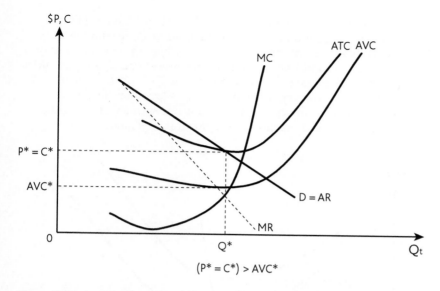

Figure 5.25 *A monopolistically competitive firm breaking even*

In Figure 5.25, the monopolistically competitive firm is breaking even. Profit maximisation occurs at a level of output Q* with a corresponding price level P* and an associated cost C*. The firm's profit per unit is zero due to the fact that P* = C*. In this case the firm is making only normal profits or breaking even. Consider, on the other hand, Figure 5.26 below, where profit maximisation occurs at a level of output Q* with a corresponding price level P* and an associated cost of C*. In this case the firm is making a loss per unit of C* − P*. The total loss incurred is equal to the loss per unit by the quantity of output produced, (C* − P*)Q*. Observe, however, that the market price is higher than the average variable cost, which implies that operating costs are being covered by the activities of the firm. In addition to which, resources are also being diverted to cover some of the fixed costs of the firm. In this case, the firm is making non-immediate shutdown losses.

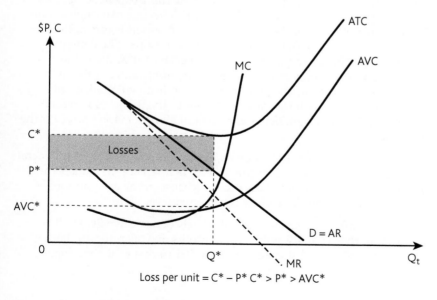

Figure 5.26 *A monopolistically competitive firm making non-immediate shutdown losses*

As with other market structures, it is possible that the typical firm in monopolistic competition can be making an immediate shutdown loss. This loss is illustrated in the diagram below where the cost per unit of the equilibrium output level C* is above the associated equilibrium price P*, so that the firm makes a loss of magnitude C* − P* (see Figure 5.27). Note in this case, however, the market price is less than the average variable cost, which implies that the firm is not even able to cover its operational costs and as such will shut down immediately.

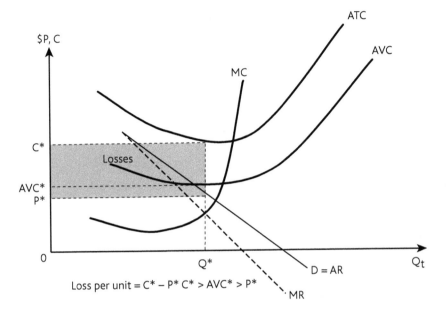

Figure 5.27 *A monopolistically competitive firm making immediate shutdown losses*

The long run in monopolistic competition

Let us assume that firms in a particular monopolistically competitive product group are making profits. In the long run this will act as a signal for resources to flow into the product group. This has two implications for the demand curve of the typical firm, as shown in Figure 5.28. The demand curve shifts leftwards and decreases in slope. The demand curve will continue to shift leftwards until each firm in the market environment earns only normal profits. The implication of this is that the profit-maximising quantity that each firm will produce will be less than that which was produced prior to the inflow of marginal suppliers. This change in demand results in a lower market price for the commodity.

In the long run, therefore, monopolistically competitive firms will operate under conditions of normal profits where the market price equals the average cost of production. This occurs because of the assumptions of perfect knowledge and weak barriers to entry.

In the long run, the typical monopolistically competitive firm will break even, that is, make only normal profits and operate with both a sub-optimal plant and spare capacity similar to that of the monopoly.

Activity 5.3

Give some examples of firms or industries that may be regarded as being monopolistically competitive.

Feedback

Examples of firms that may operate in a monopolistically competitive environment include boutiques as well as restaurants.

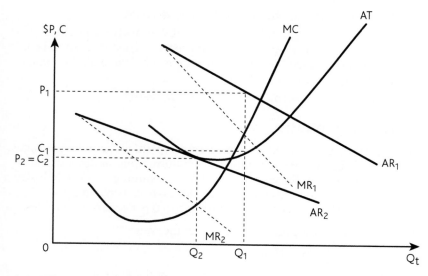

Figure 5.28 *Long-run dynamics in monopolistic competition*

Example

Marginal cost pricing and average cost pricing

Marginal cost pricing refers to the practice of setting the market price of a commodity equal to its marginal cost of production. In effect, what the producer does is charge a price that is equal to the additional cost of production, for example, assuming that the marginal cost of production for a given commodity is $1.00 and the regular selling price is $2.00. In times of falling demand, what the firm may do is to actually lower market price to marginally above its marginal cost of production, say perhaps $1.10. The firm would choose this kind of pricing approach because the incremental profit of $0.10 from the sale is preferred to no sale at all.

Average-cost pricing on the other hand is the policy of setting market prices close to average cost. Average-cost pricing is associated with sales maximisation and is therefore used by firms seeking to increase their market share. Average-cost pricing is also known as full-cost pricing or full-cost plus pricing.

Example

Cost analysis in the real world

The preceding chapters have laid the foundations of cost theory and cost analysis. In the real world, however, business costs do not always behave in a manner consistent with theory, in that the problems that arise in the real world relate to the dynamism of costs due to innovation, technology and learning by doing. In reality also, information asymmetries affect costs to the extent that planning and short- and long-run production adjustments are often necessary to be flexible to respond to environmental changes.

Innovation and technological changes improve the efficiency of production, thereby reducing the overall costs of production. Learning by doing affects costs in a similar manner.

Oligopoly

In their purest forms, monopolies and perfectly competitive firms do not exist in reality. What do exist, however, are varying degrees of market imperfection. The market type defined as an oligopoly is such an example. An oligopolistic situation exists where a few, usually large, firms characterise the market, each possessing a substantial market share.

The actual term 'oligopoly' implies the meaning of 'few', the result of which is the interdependence among the firms in the market, especially with regards to pricing policies. Though not always the case, this market structure is usually facilitative of collusion among the sellers.

The theory of oligopoly is founded upon a number of assumptions, including the following:

- The government does not intervene into the operations of the oligopolistically competitive firm in the market unless the oligopolist violates the laws of the land.
- The industry has a few large sellers and a large number of buyers.

- This market structure has strong barriers to entry.
- The firms operating in this oligopolistically competitive product group may or may not produce a homogeneous good. An example of a homogeneous good is cement, while an example of a differentiated goods motor vehicles.
- For simplicity we assume perfect knowledge exists.

Industry concentration ratio

The larger the number of firms, the more competitive the industry might seem to be. Table 5.1 provides illustrative information on firms in the soft-drink industry in the economy of 'Isles'. Assuming that the industry has a total annual volume of sales of $1,000m, is distributed across 10 firms, with the four largest accounting for 70 per cent of these sales.

We can calculate a four-firm concentration index as:

$$\frac{\sum x_i(i = 1...4)}{\sum x_i(i = 1...10)} = \frac{700}{1,000} = \frac{7}{10} \text{ of the market}$$

In this example the four-firm concentration ratio is 70 per cent. This means that the four largest firms in the industry collectively control 70 per cent of the market share.

Table 5.1 *Annual sales of 10 firms in the soft-drink industry*

Firm	Annual sales ($m)
x_1	100
x_2	150
x_3	200
x_4	250
$\sum x_1 ... x_4$	700
$\sum x_5 ... x_{10}$	300
$\sum x_1 ... x_{10}$	1,000

Herfindahl-Hirschman Index

The Herfindahl-Hirschman Index (HI) was developed to correct a number of deficiencies in the industry concentration ratio, one of which is that it fails to identify the size of the market share over which each firm has control, that is, the concentration ratio does not give any indication of the distribution of market power. Additionally, industry concentration ratios give no indication of the geographic scope of the market nor provide any information about the extent of barriers to entry or firm turnover.

This index is derived from the following formula:

$$HI = \sum_1^n S_i^2$$

where n is the number of firms and S is the market share (level of sales or quantity of output produced can also be used as alternatives to amount employed) for the ith firm in the industry. The larger the value obtained, the greater the market power by the firm.

Limitations of measures of industrial concentration

An economy characterised by a few large industries that dominate economic activity tends to be subject to peculiar vulnerabilities. Consider, for example, a resource-based economy with a large energy sector. If the energy sector accounts for some 80 per cent of GDP and 75 per cent of government revenues, then even marginal changes in the dynamics of the industry itself can result in severe shocks to an economy's standard of living. This situation can be exacerbated in cases where the country is a small country that has no control over the export commodity prices.

At the firm level, high levels of industry concentration can also result in monopoly-like situations, which have attendant negative externalities. Some of these include price fixing and predatory pricing.

Example

Albert Hirschman (born 1915)

This renowned economist has been contributing to economic literature since the middle of the last century. His first publication, in 1945, alluded to the role of economics in maintaining political power. However, Hirschman carved out his own niche in the area of development economics. His work focused on the 'hidden rationalities' in developing and developed countries, the specifics of which, he emphasised, must be considered in devising development plans for the given country.

Some of his major works include *National Power and the Structure of Foreign Trade* (1945), *The Strategy of Development* (1958) and *Rival Interpretations of Market Society; Civilizing, Destructive or Feeble* (1982).

Non-price competition (collusive behaviour)

Collusion exists when the firms agree on prices and other factors, such as output levels and market share. A cartel is a formal collusive agreement between firms in an industry.

To illustrate the effects of a cartel on output we can make reference to Figure 5.29. Ideally, what the cartel does is allow the colluding firms the opportunity to act as a single firm or monopolist. Thus the cartel as a whole will sell at the price P_0 with a per-unit cost of production C_0, which in this case allows the members of the cartel to obtain a per unit profit level of $P_0 - C_0$.

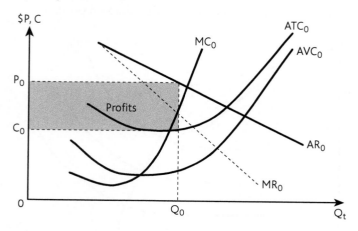

Figure 5.29 *The effect of cartelisation on price and quantity traded*

Non-collusive behaviour

Oligopolistic firms that do not collude have a demand curve such as that shown in Figure 5.30. This demand curve has two distinct parts that are respectively elastic and inelastic. With this demand curve the firm will sell a volume of output Q_0 at a price of P_0. If this firm were to increase price above P_0 then no other firm will respond, the result of which will be that the firm will lose a substantial amount of its market share. However, if the oligopolistically competitive firm were to decrease its price below P_0 all other firms in the industry, for fear of losing their market shares, would respond by reducing their prices also. The implication of this is that the fall in price will only lead to small increases in output along the inelastic segment of the demand curve.

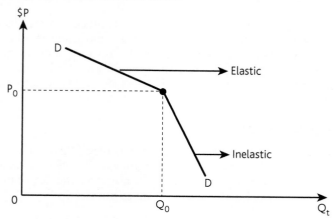

Figure 5.30 *A kinked demand curve*

Example

Organization of the Petroleum Exporting Countries (OPEC)

One of the most internationally famous cartels is that of the Organization of the Petroleum Exporting Countries (OPEC). This international organisation was established in 1960, consisting of 11 countries with the expressed mandate of stabilising the oil market. The organisation is actively involved in harmonising policies and strategic directions for the market as a whole. One of the main reasons for this degree of international collusion is to ensure that the major stakeholders in the industry obtain a reasonable rate of return on investments made in the industry.

The countries that make up OPEC include Algeria, Indonesia, Iran, Iraq, Kuwait, Libya, Nigeria, Qatar, Saudi Arabia, Venezuela and the UAE.

The non-collusive oligopolistic firm faces a kinked demand curve. The marginal revenue curve associated with this demand curve will also have a break or gap at the output level, Q_0, which corresponds to the point where the demand curve is kinked.

For a firm operating under these kinds of market conditions, the profit-maximisation output level can only be obtained at Q_0, where the MC curve can cut the MR anywhere within the break or gap. Significantly, as Figure 5.31 helps to illustrate, in spite of the fact that cost levels change, as evidenced by MC curves 0, 1 and 2, the market price of the commodity remains P_0. Oligopolistic market structures are therefore characterised by price stickiness and for this reason oligopoly firms tend to compete more on the basis of non-price competition rather than on price.

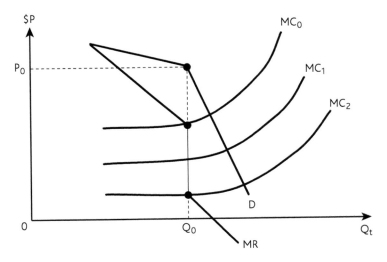

Figure 5.31 *Variable conditions market equilibrium for an oligopolist*

Game theory as applied to oligopoly

The essence of game theory is essentially reactive, in that the behaviour of rivals is taken into consideration when devising the firm's specific policy directions. Within the context of an oligopolistic market, game theory is useful in explaining individual firm behaviour especially with regards to pricing decisions. In this case, the issue of mutual interdependence arises, where the impact on the profitability of the individual firm will not only depend on its own pricing strategies but also on the pricing strategies of its rivals.

In such an environment, where intense price competition may lead to the crippling of the firms, collusion may be a definite and feasible option. Collusion may either be formal or informal. This type of environment, along with gaming theory, provides the reasoning as to why the oligopolist may infringe on the boundaries of the collusive agreement and undercut its rivals.

Oligopoly by merger

In certain cases, where collusion is deemed as illegal, firms may opt to join market forces through mergers. Merging has the effect of reducing the number of market suppliers and hence increases the degree of market imperfection by reducing the level of competition.

There are three basic types of mergers: horizontal; vertical and conglomerate.

A horizontal merger occurs when two firms in the same line and level of production join to create one company. For example, a merger between two banks, Citi Bank and the Royal Bank of Trinidad and Tobago, would be considered a horizontal merger.

A vertical merger occurs between firms at different levels of production of a given commodity. For example, such types of arrangement are common in the tourism sector between hotels and farms. There are also examples in the food processing industry, for example with the chicken processor, Nutrina Farms, steps have been taken to integrate with the suppliers of fresh chickens.

A conglomerate refers to a merger between a firm operating in one industry with firms in another industry. The Colonial Life Industry Company Ltd (Clico) is one such conglomerate existing in the Trinidad and Tobago economy. This company has diversified away from the financial and insurance sector into methanol.

> **Activity 5.4**
>
> After studying the different market structures, compare each market structure discussed based on the characteristic assumptions associated with each.

Feedback

Table 5.2 *Comparing market structures*

Characteristic assumptions	Market structures			
	Perfect competition	**Monopolistic competition**	**Oligopoly**	**Monopoly**
Number of sellers	Infinite	Large	Few	One
Ease of entry to the market	No barriers to entry	Weak barriers to entry	Relatively difficult	Very difficult
Product differentiation	No	Yes	Yes/no	Unique product
Price taker or maker	Price taker	Price maker	Price maker	Price maker
Long-run abnormal profit	No	No	Possibly	Yes but has to be aware of potential competition
Expectation of rival action	None	None	Action/reaction unless cartel is formed	No rivals

Table 5.2 gives a summary of the characteristics of each of the markets discussed throughout this chapter. With regards to the number of suppliers operating in the market, the perfectly competitive market structure is characterised by the largest number of participants as compared to the monopoly, which only has one supplier. The implication of this is that firms operating under perfectly competitive conditions are price takers, while firms in monopoly (and all other market types) are regarded as price makers.

Concerning market entry, the perfectly competitive and monopolistically competitive markets generally do not have significant barriers to entry. However, for oligopolistic and monopolistic markets, free entry is restricted.

The type of products sold also varies by market type. Products sold in perfectly competitive markets are homogeneous or standardised and therefore perfectly substitutable; however, the products sold in monopolistically competitive markets tend to be imperfectly substitutable. The products sold in oligopolistic markets can either be standardised or differentiated, while the commodity sold in monopolistic markets is unique with no close substitutes.

Oligopolies in the Caribbean

The bottled water industry is on the rise in Jamaica. This has been encouraged to a large extent by the increased health consciousness of society. In Jamaica alone, some five bottled water companies exist including Peak Bottling Company, Jamaica Drink Company Limited and Lewcan Enterprises. These companies market some 42 different brands of bottled water.

The possibility of earning long-run profits also varies by market. Perfectly and monopolistically competitive firms earn only normal profits into the long run, but because of the nature of the oligopolistic and monopolistic markets, firms can earn above normal profits well into the long run.

There is also a difference in terms of the relationship between firms in each of the markets. For example, in the perfectly competitive and monopolistically competitive markets firms tend to act independently of each other. In oligopolistic markets firms do act independently of each other in some cases, but the probability of interdependence in decision-making is much higher. In monopolistic markets there are no rivals.

Market structure and economic efficiency

Economic efficiency exists when production occurs at the minimum cost (productive efficiency) and at the socially optimum level of output (allocative efficiency). For production efficiency to exist P = minimum AC, while allocative efficiency exists when P = MC.

Perfect competition is economically efficient in the long run when the firm is making normal profits (P = minimum AC = MC). Imperfect competition on the other hand is inefficient; there is allocative inefficiency since P > MC and productive inefficiency since P > minimum AC.

Conclusion

This chapter provided an outline of the various goals of the firm, identified how profit-maximising decisions are made and introduced the concepts of the different types of market structures. The various characteristics of these market structures were also detailed within the context of pricing and output decisions.

This chapter also introduced the concepts and associated measures of industrial concentration.

Key points

- There are several types of market structure that exist today. Market structures refer to the conditions under which a product or service is bought and sold.
- There are four main market types that are covered by this study guide; these are perfect competition, monopoly, monopolistic competition and oligopoly.
- Perfect competition refers to a market structure that is characterised by the absence of rivalry. In its purest sense, the term 'rivalry' is associated with competition and as such firms in this market structure do not compete against each other for market share or customer loyalty as in other market structures.
- A monopoly is a market structure that is characterised by only one seller that produces a commodity (or service) for which there are no close substitutes.
- An oligopolistic situation exists where a few, usually large, firms characterise the market, each possessing a substantial market share.
- The non-collusive oligopolistic firm faces a kinked demand curve. The marginal revenue curve associated with this demand curve will also have a break or gap, at the output level, which corresponds to the point where the demand curve is kinked.

6 Market failure

Content

- Inclusion of discussion of Pareto efficiency
- Examples of private goods, public goods and merit goods
- Discussion of issues of rivalry and exclusion
- Social costs, private costs, social benefits, private benefits, external costs, external benefits – use of graphical representations
- Divergence of social costs and social benefits and efficiency – use of graphical representations
- Deadweight loss including verbal and graphical representations
- Causes of market failure:
  - Monopoly
  - Public goods and merit goods
  - Externalities: positive and negative
  - Divergence between social and private costs and social and private benefits
  - Imperfect information
  - Asymmetric information: adverse selection and moral hazard
  - Open access to resources
  - Lack of property rights (squatting, streams, ocean)
  - Non-existence of markets (for trading)

Efficiency

In economics there are various dimensions of efficiency. Efficiency is concerned with the optimal production and distribution of scarce factors of production. Economic efficiency is also known as Pareto efficiency or Pareto optimality. The term was named after Vilfredo Pareto the Italian economist who pioneered studies in resource allocation and income distribution.

The concept of Pareto efficiency can be illustrated as follows. Given a set of different combinations of outcomes for a group of individuals, switching from one alternative combination to another that makes at least one individual better off without making another worse off, is known as a Pareto improvement or a Pareto optimal move. A given allocation is therefore Pareto optimal when no further Pareto improvements are possible. Alternatively, Pareto efficiency occurs when it is not possible to improve the allocation to one outcome without reducing allocations to any other outcome.

Pareto efficiency is best illustrated along the boundary of the production possibility frontier (PPF). Such that, increasing production of the x-axis good or service requires a fall in the production of the y-axis good or service.

Private goods

A private good in economics is defined as any good that is *excludable* and *rivalrous*. The excludable property of such goods relate to the fact that it is possible to prevent consumers from consuming them. The rivalrous nature of the good implies that the consumption of the same good cannot occur simultaneously by more than one consumer. In this regard, private goods are very different from public goods, which are by nature non-rivalrous. An example of a private good can be bread. Consider that bread eaten by one person cannot be consumed by another (rivalrous nature), coupled with the fact that a bakery reserves the right to refuse to trade a loaf (excludable nature).

Public goods

Public goods are non-rivalrous in nature. This means that several people can consume the good at the same time. A hamburger is a private good on the grounds that it is consumed by one person at a time, while a public park offers benefits to several users at the same time.

Public goods are also non-excludable: it is difficult or impossible to exclude other users. So, with a national defence system, for example, all citizens benefit, including non-nationals living in the country, even though they may not be paying taxes. Even more, the cost of this public good to a new migrant worker is zero. The free-market system therefore fails in that some individuals can enjoy these goods at no economic cost. This is known as the 'free-rider' problem.

Merit goods

Merit goods refer to those goods and services that the free market, working through the price mechanism, would only be able to provide in limited quantities. In this regard, a government wishing to see more merit goods on the market (e.g. secondary-school education) may intervene and increase the existing supply by engaging in the production and supply of this commodity.

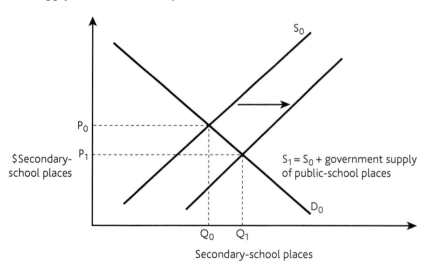

Figure 6.1 *Market for secondary-school places*

With a merit good at the price P_0 the free market will produce Q_0. Let us assume the relevant good is secondary-school places. If government believes that from a developmental perspective it requires a greater number of its citizens to benefit from secondary-school education then it can intervene on the market and increase the existing supply by $Q_1 - Q_0$

by building public secondary schools. The net effect is that the overall cost of secondary-school education falls to P_1 with Q_1 places utilised.

Private costs and social costs, private benefits and social benefits

Private costs refers to the costs borne by the individual decision-maker. Note that these costs are based on actual market prices. For example the cost of a car.

Social costs refer to the total costs borne by the community for a particular decision. Social costs in this regard are equal to the sum of private costs plus the externalities faced by third parties, associated with a particular decision. In this case also, costs are based on market prices and opportunity costs are also considered. The social cost of building a highway includes cost of resources, noise pollution and dust pollution that affects asthmatics who live close to the construction sites.

Private benefits refer to the returns that accrue to the individual decision-maker, for example the aesthetic value of a garden to a homemaker. External benefits on the other hand refer to the desirable results that accure to third parties of a particular decision, for example neighbours having access to security lighting provided by someone else. Social benefits refer to the total benefits enjoyed by a community for a particular decision. Social benefits include private benefits and external benefits.

Competitive markets and efficiency

Goods and services are produced by the market, the government, as well as by the bounties of nature. Society values goods and services produced by the market differently from goods produced by government and goods produced by the bounties of nature. As a consequence, certain types of goods may be overproduced or underproduced. Take merit goods for example (as in figure 6.1), the market underproduces the optimum level of merit goods and as such governments intervene to increase output of such goods in order to expand access.

Governments may also intervene in some markets to expand the output produced, as is the case with merit goods, or may intervene to reduce the amount of goods produced, as with demerit goods. Alternatively, said governments intervene to increase the production of those goods that have positive externalities and intervene to decrease the production of those goods that have negative externalities.

The theory of the firm indicates that profits are maximised, or in other words, private producer benefits are maximised at the point where marginal benefit (marginal revenue) equals the marginal cost of production. To determine the quantity of output that is optimal for society as a whole, social benefits and costs must also be considered. Societal efficiency occurs where the marginal social benefit derived from the production of a good is exactly equal to its marginal social cost.

Illustratively, therefore, in a situation where negative externalities occur as a result of a particular production decision, marginal social costs tend to be higher than marginal private costs. Alternatively, when positive externalities accrue, marginal social benefits are greater than marginal private benefits.

Activity 6.1

Distinguish between positive and negative externalities.

Feedback

An externality occurs when there is a difference between the social costs and private costs and the private benefits and social benefits. A negative externality occurs when the marginal social costs exceed the marginal private costs; it is most associated with an overproduction of a good. An example of a negative externality is the environmental pollution that occurs from factories. A positive externality occurs when the marginal social benefits exceed the marginal private benefits that usually occur when the good produced by the market is lower than the optimal level required by society.

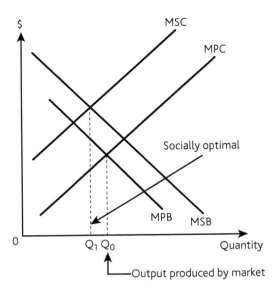

Figure 6.2 *Positive and negative externalities*

Deadweight loss

Deadweight loss refers to the market inefficiency caused by any type of intervention. Deadweight losses can occur when price floors, price ceilings, taxes or subsidies are imposed on a market. Figure 6.3 illustrates these losses.

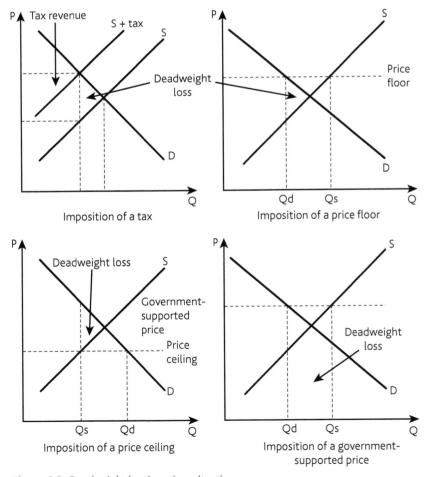

Figure 6.3 *Deadweight loss in various situations*

Market failure

Market failure arises when the economy is unable to produce an efficient level of output and as such there is either underproduction or overproduction taking place. Market failure is a prominent feature of the free-market system.

Causes of market failure

When the market does not result in an efficient allocation of scarce resources, we say that the market has failed. Market failure emerges in an environment in which the decision-makers are not exposed to the full costs and benefits associated with their economic activity. Market failure principally occurs when the price of a commodity is not determined by the interaction of its demand and supply curves. If the market conditions that promote the efficient allocation of scarce resources do not exist, then the net benefit from a particular economic activity will not be fully realised.

In markets that work efficiently, the price on the market is determined by the interaction of demand and supply, implying that decision-making is conditioned by the collective actions of many independent consumers and suppliers. In some free markets, however, for a variety of reasons powerful buyers and sellers can emerge. When a single buyer or single group of buyers dominate a market it is possible that they will try to establish a price below marginal costs. While if a seller dominates the market, it is possible they will try to set a price above marginal costs. For market efficiency, price should be equal to marginal costs, but in these types of circumstances there is a distortion between marginal cost and prices. Some of the other specific reasons why market failure may occur in a given market can include the following.

Formation of monopolies

Imperfect market conditions also lead to the development of monopolies. Monopolies emerge due to information asymmetries and other types of barriers to entry. Monopolies can potentially be exploitative towards consumers given the specific market characteristics under which these firms operate. Monopolies tend to sell relatively price inelastic commodities as the market structure has no close substitutes.

Existence of externalities

Externalities often arise out of the fact that there is a divergence between social and private costs and social and private benefits. Negative externalities exist when marginal social cost exceeds marginal private cost. Negative externalities are often associated with overproduction of a good. Environmental pollution is one type of negative externality for which the social cost incurred far exceeds the private cost.

There are also positive externalities. Positive externalities accrue when marginal social benefit exceeds marginal private benefit and are often associated with a situation where the good produced by the market is lower than the optimal level required by society.

The existence of market failure does not necessarily require government intervention as this can often make the situation worse. Nevertheless, public sector involvement is often the main way of dealing with market failure.

Information asymmetry

Asymmetric information occurs when some economic agents know more than others.

Example

The market for cars

If an individual buys a car for $50,000 drives it for 80 miles and then decides to sell, he may not be able to get more than $40,000.

The car has lost value not only because it was driven for 80 miles but because of the asymmetric information involved. The asymmetric information in this case is that the seller knows more about the car than the buyer. For example, the new buyer will always be guessing as to why the current owner is selling.

Keynes' view on market failure: information asymmetry

Keynes alluded to the importance of the role of the state, primarily because he identified that markets do not function efficiently, as information asymmetries and market imperfections arise.

Keynes insisted on state intervention in situations where the markets either underproduced merit goods or overproduced demerit goods. He also suggested a role for the state in the production of public goods, which are not produced by the private sector. He identified externalities as another type of market failure, defined as both the negative and positive effects of the activity of an economic agent on other agents in the economy.

Keynes insisted on specific intervention, such as taxation and subsidies, to encourage production of those commodities that are produced in quantities below the socially optimal level, and discourage the production of those commodities that are produced in quantities above the socially optimal level.

Adverse selection

Adverse selection is the term used in economics to illustrate how information asymmetry can negatively affect market outcomes. In particular, either buyers or sellers lack complete information so that they can adversely select 'bad' products or 'bad' customers respectively.

For example, organisations and institutions from which credit can be accessed now have facilities where information on the quality of the applicant can be accessed and disseminated. Information is shared among organisations in this industry through computerised credit histories. This facility is now being widely used to reduce the extent of information asymmetry when firms negotiate transactions with consumers.

The Computerized Credit Histories is a facility that can be accessed to determine the creditworthiness of an applicant. It gives a detailed outlook of the individual's credit history and credit report. This type of information is essential in helping the lending institution make the most optimal decision in order to minimise its own risk of losses.

Moral hazard

Moral hazard behaviour occurs when an insured party has the ability to influence the probability of the event on which payments are made. Consider Figure 6.4.

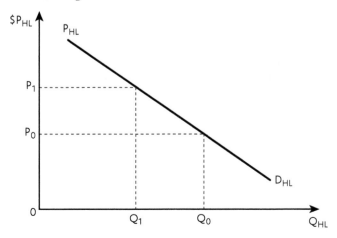

Figure 6.4 *Moral hazard consumption*

Assume that the market for medical services is such that at the price level of $\$P_1$ the quantity traded of health care is Q_1. With health insurance $\$P_1 - P_0$ is provided by the health insurers. The consumption of $Q_0 - Q_1$ extra units of health care represents moral hazard consumption. By lowering the cost of a commodity the allocation of resources to that commodity is affected.

Implications of asymmetric information

In a world of information asymmetry, markets fail, resulting in ill-informed decisions by consumers. Ultimately, in such situations consumers lose out.

▪ Asymmetric information and health care: People over 65 years generally find it difficult to get insurance as older people are more prone to a wider range of illnesses. But the price of insurance does not necessarily increase to reflect this greater risk because people who buy insurance generally know more about their health than the insurance companies. People who are ill or potentially ill are more likely to choose insurance than healthier people. This means that of all the insured people, the proportion of people who are unhealthy is relatively higher than the healthy ones.

As the proportion of unhealthy people in the pool of insured people increases, there will be an increase in demand for insurance claims. The price of insurance will need to increase even further. As the price of insurance increases, healthy people will choose less, *ceteris paribus*.

▪ Asymmetric information and the financial sector: A credit card allows the holder to access credit without collateral. Many people carry credit cards from several different financial institutions. Ideally, credit card companies will prefer to charge a high rate of interest to low-quality borrowers and a low rate of interest to high-quality borrowers. Unfortunately, because credit card companies are forced to charge the same rate of interest to all borrowers, a greater quantum of low-quality borrowers participate at a low rate of interest. When these low-quality borrowers default on their credit, the price of credit, the rate of interest, increases. This drives high-quality borrowers out of the market, so that it eventually becomes dominated by low-quality borrowers. This creates a cycle that can destroy the market for credit.

Public and merit goods

Public goods are non-rivalrous and non-excludable and, as such, the market that is profit driven does not generally produce such goods. Regarding merit goods, however, the market does not produce enough of this type of good. To correct for the shortfalls in market production, the government intervenes to produce public goods and to increase the supply of merit goods available to society.

Open access to resources

There are some goods that are non-excludable but rivalrous; these are common goods or common-pool resources. For such goods, consumers have open access to common goods such as fish stocks and public health care. Markets for such goods are non-existent. For example, sea eggs (white sea urchins) are a delicacy in Barbados. Years of over-reaping have led to the decimation of the sea egg populations.

Lack of property rights

The lack of property rights may result in a situation where infringement or the unauthorised use of property or even intellectual property may

---

Activity 6.2
What is the difference between adverse selection and moral hazard?

Feedback

Adverse selection occurs when there is asymmetric information between the buyer and the seller. This means that either the buyer or the seller lacks complete information and the information they have can cause them to adversely select bad products. For instance, the seller can be at a disadvantage for selling insurance if the buyer knows more information about his risk and withholds that information.

A situation of moral hazard can exist when people who are insured, for example, take greater risks than they normally do because they know that they are insured. Thus they have control over the probability of an event on which payments are to be made.

occur. Weak institutional support and enforcement may also result in this type of situation. Examples include squatters who reside on either public or private property, fishermen who fish in the territorial waters of another country because fish populations have migrated away from the water of the fishermen's country.

Conclusion

This chapter reviews the concept of economic efficiency. Examples of private goods, public goods and merit goods are also discussed. The concepts of social cost, private cost, social benefit and private benefit were also included. The issue of deadweight losses and market failure were also addressed.

Key points

- In economics there are various dimensions of efficiency. Efficiency is concerned with the optimal production and distribution of scarce factors of production. Economic efficiency is also known as Pareto efficiency or Pareto optimality.

- A private good in economics is defined as any good that is *excludable* and *rivalrous*.

- Public goods are non-rivalrous in nature. Public goods are also non-excludable, meaning that it is difficult or impossible to exclude other users.

- Merit goods refer to those goods and services that the free market, working through the price mechanism, would only be able to provide in limited quantities.

- Private costs refer to the costs borne by the individual decision-maker. Social costs refer to the total costs borne by the commumity for a particular decision.

- Private benefits refer to the returns that accrue to the individual decision-maker. Social benefits refer to the total benefits enjoyed by a community for a particular decision. Social benefits include private benefits and external benefits.

- Deadweight loss refers to the market inefficiency caused by any type of intervention. Deadweight losses can occur when price floors, price ceilings, taxes or subsidies are imposed on a market.

- Market failure arises when the economy is unable to produce an efficient level of output and, as such, there is either underproduction or overproduction taking place. Market failure is a prominent feature of the free-market system.

7 Intervention

Content

- Measures used by government to control market failure:
    - Regulation
    - Antitrust policy
    - Taxation
    - Privatisation and deregulation
    - State ownership
    - Subsidies
    - Legislation
    - Market creation (tradable permits)
  - Pros and cons of government intervention:
    - Merits and demerits
    - Effectiveness of intervention in Caribbean societies (effect of small size in relation to policy making)
- Private sector intervention:
  - Corporate code of conduct
  - Corporate social responsibility
  - Voluntary agreements
  - Corporate ethics

Government response to market failure

The existence of market failure is a principal reason for government intervention, as it is the responsibility of the government to protect consumers and the disadvantaged in society.

When the market fails, there are a number of options available to any government to correct the problem, including the imposition of taxes (indirect, *ad valorem* (VAT) and specific), subsidies, and minimum and maximum price legislation to name a few.

Taxation

Indirect taxes

Indirect taxes are placed on goods and services. They raise the cost of consumption and so reduce consumer demand. Table 7.1 provides an illustration of the trends in some of the excise duties collected by the government in Trinidad and Tobago from rum, beer and cigarettes for the period 1988–2001. Excise duties are taxes on the imports of specific commodities, including rum and spirits. As can be seen, while tax revenues doubled in aggregate, revenues from rum increased just about fourfold while revenues from beer increased threefold. Revenues from cigarettes increased by approximately the same proportion as those of aggregate revenues.

Table 7.1 *Central government revenues from excise duties on rum, beer and cigarettes in Trinidad and Tobago, TT$m, 1988–2001*

	Tax revenue	Excise duties	Rum	Beer	Cigarettes
1988	3,928.9	309.8	26.4	34.8	42.8
1989	3,957.5	388.5	24.1	513.0	76.9
1990	4,755.6	472.5	61.7	76.0	55.3
1991	5,646.2	415.9	69.2	76.7	55.8
1992	5,234.6	668.6	134.5	83.3	85.4
1993	5,678.6	802.2	97.1	92.6	91.0
1994	6,163.7	667.6	87.7	99.6	88.3
1995	7,000.0	603.9	95.7	86.3	85.7
1996	7,906.4	610.0	91.1	87.6	94.7
1997	7,566.8	757.8	108.7	93.1	98.6
1998	7,566.8	582.4	66.6	65.7	89.0
1999	5,907.5	892.0	89.9	89.7	122.7
2000	9,644.7	800.7	100.0	95.5	123.8
2001	10,093.2	822.3	95.1	106.4	125.1

Source: Annual Economic Survey (various issues)

Specific taxes

A specific tax has the same impact on economic activity as a rise in the cost of production. Specific taxes are a significant source of revenue for the government but they are difficult to administer and may vary with changes to the business cycle.

Feedback

> **Activity 7.1**
>
> Discuss some of the reasons why governments may impose indirect taxes.

Governments impose indirect taxes for four main reasons:

- To raise revenue. In Trinidad and Tobago in 1990, VAT was imposed by the government in an attempt to help consolidate the fiscal revenue intake of the government in the wake of weakening oil revenues. The territory's economy was on its way to recovering from the economic depression of the 1980s, the period over which oil revenues plummeted and overall standards of living in the country declined. Over this period, incomes fell and, as such, the revenues earned from direct taxation methods fell considerably. With the implementation of a Structural Adjustment Programme, the taxation system was overhauled to capture revenue from indirect sources, such as consumption or value added taxes.

- To reduce consumption and/or production. In order to do this, the price elasticity of demand should tend towards infinity, that is, demand must be elastic. Indirect taxes, such as the value added tax, have the effect of increasing prices charged to consumers. This would result, according to the fundamental laws of economics, in a fall in consumer demand and an increase in producer supply. If targeted towards reducing consumption, the effects of the imposition of the tax will have a greater impact if demand is elastic as consumers will be more responsive to price changes.

- To modify welfare levels. Goods with negative externalities are overproduced and underpriced. Indirect taxation can be used to curtail the production of these types of goods and services. For example, if the government wishes to affect the production of a demerit good, such as pornography, this activity can be heavily taxed. The result of a heavier amount of taxation is that the price of this commodity will increase and the quantity demanded will fall.

- Taxation to reduce income inequities. In a situation where there are wide income classes or groups, taxation may be utilised to put more disposable income in the hands of the lower income groups. Progressive taxation is one of the most widely used income redistribution methods. Progressive taxation systems are characterised by progressively higher rates of taxation on higher income groups.

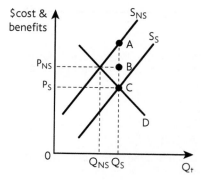

Figure 7.1 *The effects on equilibrium when a subsidy is imposed*

Subsidies

In order to encourage the production of goods that are underproduced by the economic system, a government may grant subsidies. How does a subsidy impact on the market? A subsidy shifts the supply curve downwards and to the right, and so may be viewed as a negative tax.

In the case of Figure 7.1, the effect of the subsidy is to shift the supply curve rightwards from S_{NS} to S_S and to encourage a fall in price from P_{NS} to P_S and thus an increase in the equilibrium quantity traded from Q_{NS} to Q_S. The value of the subsidy is AC, of which AB is the gain per unit of output for the supplier and BC is the reduction in costs that the consumer receives. As before, the magnitude of AB in relation to BC depends on the relative elasticities of supply and demand curves.

For instance, let us assume that demand was perfectly inelastic, represented by the vertical demand curve D (see Figure 7.2).

In this case, with a subsidy, the price falls from PNS to PS but the quantity traded does not change, so that the subsidy benefits only the consumer. In the reverse case of perfectly elastic demand, as illustrated in Figure 7.3, the rightward shift in supply benefits the supplier only.

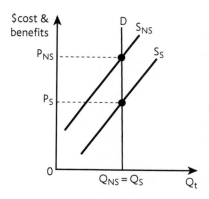

Figure 7.2 *The effects of a unit subsidy on perfectly inelastic demand*

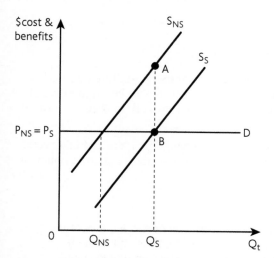

Figure 7.3 *The effects of a unit subsidy on perfectly elastic demand*

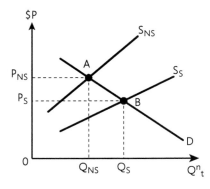

Figure 7.4 *The effects of an* ad valorem *subsidy on price and quantity demanded*

Activity 7.2

Discuss some of the reasons why subsidies may be given.

The value of the subsidy is AB. Subsidies can also be *ad valorem* in nature. *Ad valorem* subsidies shift the supply curve rightwards but not in a parallel manner.

In Figure 7.4, the *ad valorem* subsidy shifts the supply curve to the right causing output to expand from Q_{NS} to Q_S and price to fall from P_{NS} to P_S.

Feedback

Subsidies are given to assist the poor, in order to help them attain levels of consumption of goods and services that are considered desirable by the government. Subsidies are also given to producers to help reduce their per unit costs of production, especially if they have positive externalities.

In small, highly open developing economies, subsidies are offered to private investors for the following reasons:

- To preserve domestic job levels: this helps to reduce the attendant social evils that go with rising unemployment levels, such as crime. Subsidies have the effect of reducing the cost of producing goods and services, and so help to produce an expansion in the output of benefiting industries.

- To protect strategic industries: governments often grant subsidies to firms in certain industries, because of their central importance to the country's security. For example, some countries strive to produce their own energy sector products so that in times of international instability their economies do not grind to a halt. In this case subsidies are used to encourage resources to remain in a certain type of productive activity because in some cases the continued production has greater social and national benefit in terms of reducing vulnerability to external circumstances.

- To compete with foreign firms: some firms are granted subsidies so they can compete with other firms from other countries that benefit from subsidies from their home country government.

- To support technological change: governments sometimes subsidise the firms involved in research, so as to help the technological advancement of the country. It is often the case that governments are unable to actively engage in research and development (R&D), as such they often subsidise the process for firms and industries that are independently carrying out R&D. Subsidising R&D increases the rate at which technological advancement and innovations are made.

Regulation and antitrust legislation

Monopolies are often regarded as evidence of market failure due to the fact that there is the potential for such institutions to be exploitative of consumers. In addition, monopolies produce a less than socially optimal level of output.

To prevent the formation of monopolies through mergers and takeovers, the government legislates and regulates in the form of antitrust policy and antitrust laws.

State ownerships

In markets that do not facilitate more than one provider, it is often the case that such providers are natural monopolies and as such the government becomes involved in the production of goods and services. In the provision of utilities this type of situation is prominent.

In Trinidad and Tobago, the provision of water, electricity and telecommunication services is provided by the government. Some of the other essential services that are provided by the government include education and health.

Privatisation and deregulation

Privatisation refers to the selling of state-owned enterprises to the private sector, while deregulation refers to the reduction or removal of 'red tape' and bureaucracy associated with running state-owned enterprises. The current trend is towards privatisation and deregulation of governmental organisations or state-owned organisations. This comes as a result of the proven inefficiencies associated with the public sector, coupled with the move towards the reduced role of the state.

Legislation

Legislation can be used to reduce the extent of negative externalities in some markets. For example, governments can introduce legislation that could ensure that waste effluent does not seep into waterways, streams and rivers and, in the event that such instances do occur, that these companies would be responsible for the costs incurred as a consequence.

Market creation (tradable permits)

Tradable permits relate to the sale of goods and services that have an associated negative externality, such as pollution. Under a tradable permit system firms are allowed to engage in trade below a certain level as defined by their permit. This type of system keeps a check on the production and distribution of goods that can potentially have significant negative effects on the environment.

Pros and cons of government intervention

Table 7.2 gives a summary of some of the issues regarding government intervention. In particular, the table below lists some of the advantages and disadvantages associated with government intervention.

Example

TTPost

TTPost, the Postal Service Company operating in Trinidad and Tobago, is a private sector company from Australia which has managed to improve the efficiency and effectiveness in delivery of the postal services in Trinidad and Tobago.

Table 7.2 *Issues regarding government Intervention*

Intervention	Advantages	Disadvantages
Regulation	Can be used to positively impact individual, household and firm behaviour	Enforcement requires continuous assessment and evaluation, which may translate into high operation and administration costs
Antitrust policy	Promoting competition in the marketplace benefits consumers	Market may not be large enough to allow profitability of more than one firm, e.g. where natural monopolies emerge
Taxation	Government revenue	Additional cost associated with administration of the tax
State ownership	Ensures access by all	Operations associated with high levels of bureaucracy and corruption State ownership is often associated with high levels of inefficiency
Subsidies	Increases domestic production	May be unsustainable in the long run

Intervention	Advantages	Disadvantages
Legislation	Can be used to positively impact individual, household and firm behaviour	Enforcement is difficult and costly in some cases
Market creation	Controls for the production of goods and services that may be associated with negative externalities	Permits can be abused

Example

Government intervention in Caribbean societies

There are several examples of state intervention in the Caribbean. Caribbean economies are developing economies and, as such, the state plays a major role as the driving force towards economic growth and development. In many Caribbean economies the state remains the largest employer, owns enterprises, controls utility companies, administers taxation and enforces laws and regulations.

For example, in the Trinidad and Tobago economy some 45 per cent of the labour force is employed by the state, and there are more than 10 state boards that oversee the operations of state-run companies and other utilities providers.

Private sector intervention to correct market failure

As discussed above, the government intervenes to correct market failure. It is also possible that the private sector can engage in activities that may ultimately work to correct market failure. Some of these activities include:

- Corporate code of conduct or ethics: A corporate code of conduct refers to specific company policy statements that seek to define the standards for its conduct. These codes can take a number of formats and address any number of issues, including employee compensation and worker rights. The standards include not only marketing and selling but also product safety and product quality, as well as compliance with local laws and environmental issues. When there is information asymmetry, the consumers will not know as much about the product as the supplier. By following high standards for production and providing information, firms will reduce this market failure. Although the implementation of these codes depends on the company itself, over time, if these are enforced, it can contribute to the company's public image, which ultimately affects its sales and market share.

- Corporate social responsibility (CSR): CSR refers to the deliberate inclusion of issues pertaining to the community into its corporate decision-making within the context of its triple bottom line (people, planet, profit). Via CSR, businesses accept responsibility for the impact of their operations and other activities on the environment, their consumers, their employees, community and other stakeholders. CSR therefore ultimately reduces the negative externalities associated with the production of some goods and so can be used to enhance a firm's public image. Firms can practice CSR by using green technology and other production methods, such as those based on solar power.

- Voluntary agreements: A voluntary agreement (VA) or company voluntary agreement (CVA) is a legally binding agreement that a firm can undertake with its creditors regarding the repayment of its debt, for example. CVAs can enable a firm to increase cash flow in the short run, which can be used for example to augment a firm's capital base. CVAs can also prevent large-scale downsizing in cases where businesses are being pressured into bankruptcy.

  Government and firms can also enter VAs, for example whereby firms agree to reduce pollutants. These agreements are legally binding. This type of VA is often preferred to regulation since it is less costly. Firms can gradually reduce emissions according to agreed timelines. Inspectors will monitor the progress of the reductions in the emissions. For example, a firm that releases hot water into the sea can affect coral reefs adversely by causing bleaching. The firm can voluntarily agree to have the water run off to a catchment area where it will cool and become brackish before it reaches the sea.

- Corporate ethics: Corporate ethics refers to the standard of conduct by which a company interacts with its employees, its customers and other stakeholders. Corporate ethics provide a code of behavioural norms, which ultimately influence a company's public image.

Conclusion

This chapter provided a review of the various measures used by the government as well as by the private sector to correct market failure.

Key points

▪ The existence of market failure is a principal reason for government intervention, as it is the responsibility of the government to protect consumers and the disadvantaged in society.

▪ When the market fails, there are a number of options available to any government to correct the problem, including the imposition of taxes (indirect, *ad valorem* and specific), subsidies, and minimum and maximum price legislation to name a few.

▪ It is also possible that the private sector can engage in activities that may ultimately work to correct market failure.

End test

Consider the data shown in the table below, which relates to questions 1–3.

Quantity of toy cars produced	1	2	3	4	5
Fixed cost	200	200	200	200	200
Variable cost	300	500	700	450	1,300

1 What is the AFC of producing three toy cars?
  a $200/3$ c $700/3$
  b $1,500/3$ d $900/3$

2 What is the ATC of producing three toy cars?
  a $200/3$ c $700/3$
  b $1,500/3$ d $900/3$

3 What is the MC of producing the third toy car?
  a 100   c 300
  b 200   d 400

4 In the diagram below, at what level of output should the perfectly competitive firm produce in order to maximise its profits?

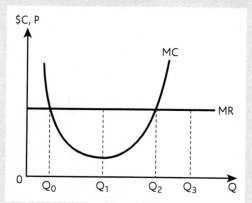

a Q_0
b Q_1
c Q_2
d Q_3

5 The perfectly competitive firm in the diagram below is making losses. At which price level would it be operating?

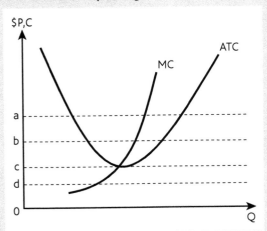

6 Consider the diagram below and answer the question that follows.

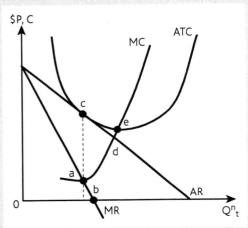

For a monopolist to maximise profits will it operate at a, b, c or d?

7 In the diagram below, monopoly profits are given by the area bounded by which of the following?

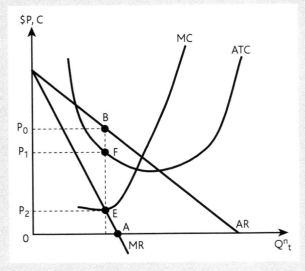

a $P_0 P_1 F B$
b $P_1 O A F$
c $P_0 O A F$
d $P_2 O A E$

8   In the long run, the monopolistically competitive firm makes:

   a   normal profits   **c**   losses

   b   huge supernormal profits   **d**   no significant supernormal profits

9   In the long run, a monopolistically competitive firm is characterised by which of the following?

   a   spare capacity   **c**   overused capacity

   b   optimal capacity   **d**   none of the above

10 An oligopolistic market structure is characterised by which of the following?

   a   many large sellers   **c**   a few large sellers

   b   a few small sellers   **d**   many small sellers

11 Which of the following reasons can result in market failure in an economy?

   a   tall trees   **c**   droughts

   b   heavy rainfall   **d**   pollution of the rivers

12 If someone owns a honeybee farm, then the neighbour next door growing flowers would realise:

   a   a positive externality   **c**   no externality

   b   a negative externality   **d**   an increase in costs

13 An *ad valorem* tax can be defined as:

   a   a fixed charge on every unit sold   **c**   a subsidy paid to firms

   b   a percentage charge on the price level **d**   a subsidy paid to consumers

14 The government wishes to subsidise pre-school education in a rural community. The reason for this is because the government is of the persuasion that pre-school education is:

   a   underproduced   **c**   overproduced

   b   underpriced   **d**   overpriced

Consider the diagram below and answer questions 15 and 16 which follow. It shows that with the imposition of a tax, supply shifts from S_0 to S_1.

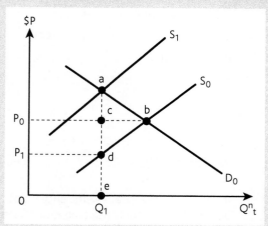

15 Which of the following represents the tax burden for consumers?

   a   ac   **c**   cd

   b   bc   **d**   de

16 Which of the following represents the tax burden for producers?

   a   ab   **c**   cd

   b   bc   **d**   de

17 Full funding of tertiary-level education is an example of a government:

    a tax   **c** subsidy

    b tariff   **d** loan

18 Monopolistic competition and the theory of perfect competition are similar in which of the following respects?

    a Long-run economic profits are zero.

    b Price is greater than marginal cost.

    c Price is equivalent to minimum average cost.

    d In the long run, firms can make supernormal profits.

19 If a monopolistically competitive firm is making profits in the short run, what would happen to the industry in the long run?

    a Resources would flow out of the product group and supply would fall.

    b Resources will flow into the product group and supply would rise.

    c Firms will form a cartel to protect their profits.

    d Individual firms would set up barriers to entry to maintain their short-run profits.

20 Which of the following statements is true about monopolistic competition in the long run?

    a Monopolistic competition achieves allocative efficiency because price equals average cost in long-run equilibrium.

    b In the long run, price equals marginal cost but exceeds average cost, causing the monopolistic competitor to fall short of allocative efficiency.

    c In the long run, allocative efficiency is not achieved in monopolistic competition because price is greater than marginal cost.

    d Allocative efficiency is achieved in monopolistic competition because economic profits are eliminated in the long run.

End test feedback

1	a	$200/3$
2	d	$900/3$
3	b	200
4	c	Q_2
5	d	
6	a	
7	a	$P_0 P_1 F B$
8	a	normal profits
9	a	spare capacity
10	c	a few large sellers
11	d	pollution of the rivers

12	a	a positive externality
13	b	a percentage charge on the price level
14	a	underproduced
15	a	ac
16	c	cd
17	c	subsidy
18	a	Long-run economic profits are zero.
19	b	Resources will flow into the product group and supply would rise.
20	c	In the long run, allocative efficiency is not achieved in monopolistic competition because price is greater than marginal cost.

Tutor-marked assignment

1   What is the main goal of the firm according to the neoclassical school of economics?

2   Explain the term 'market structures'.

3   Compare each of the following market types: perfect competition, monopolistic competition, oligopoly, monopoly.

4   Which market structure is economically efficient?

5   What is a deadweight loss?

6   Explain the term 'market failure'.

7   How does the government respond to market failure?

8   Why is the existence of monopolies regarded as evidence of market failure?

9   List three ways in which the private sector responds to market failure.

10 Explain the term 'corporate social responsibility'.

Feedback

1   Profit maximisation.

2   Market structures refer to the conditions under which a product or service is bought and sold.

3   The following table can be used as a point of reference.

Characteristic assumptions	Market structures			
	Perfect competition	**Monopolistic competition**	**Oligopoly**	**Monopoly**
Number of sellers	Infinite	Large	Few	One
Ease of entry to the market	No barriers to entry	Weak barriers to entry	Relatively difficult	Very difficult
Product differentiation	No	Yes	Yes/no	Unique product
Price taker or maker	Price taker	Price maker	Price maker	Price maker
Long-run abnormal profit	No	No	Possibly	Yes but has to be aware of potential competition
Expectation of rival action	None	None	Action/reaction unless cartel is formed	No rivals

4   Economic efficiency exists when production occurs at the minimum cost (productive efficiency) and at the socially optimum level of output (allocative efficiency). For production efficiency to exist $P = $ minimum AC while allocative efficiency exists when $P = MC$. Firms operating under perfect competition tend in the long run to be efficient.

5   Deadweight loss refers to the market inefficiency caused by any type of intervention. Deadweight losses can occur when price floors, price ceilings, taxes or subsidies are imposed on a market.

6 Market failure arises when the economy is unable to produce an efficient level of output and, as such, there is either underproduction or overproduction taking place. Market failure is a prominent feature of the free-market system.

7 The existence of market failure is a principal reason for government intervention, as it is the responsibility of the government to protect consumers and the disadvantaged in society. When the market fails, there are a number of options available to any government to correct the problem, including the imposition of taxes (indirect, *ad valorem* and specific), subsidies, and minimum and maximum price legislation to name a few.

8 Monopolies are often regarded as evidence of market failure due to the fact that there is the potential for such institutions to be exploitative of consumers.

9 The private sector responds to market failure through:

a its corporate code of ethics

b voluntary agreements

c corporate social responsibility.

10 Corporate social responsibility (CSR) refers to the deliberate inclusion of issues pertaining to the community into its corporate decision-making within the context of its triple bottom line (people, planet, profit). Via CSR, businesses accept responsibility for the impact of their operations and other activities on the environment, their consumers, their employees, community and other stakeholders. CSR therefore ultimately reduces the negative externalities associated with the production of some goods and so can be used to enhance a firm's public image.

8 Module 3: Distribution theory
Demand and supply factors

General objectives

On completion of this module, you should be able to:

understand what accounts for the returns that accrue to the owners of the factors of production

appreciate the issues surrounding poverty and the measures used to alleviate poverty

develop skills in applying microeconomic analysis to critical social issues involving income inequality.

Specific objectives

You should be able to:

explain the rewards of the factors of production

explain the concept of derived demand

outline the marginal productivity theory

apply the marginal productivity theory to the demand for land, capital and labour

analyse the factors affecting the supply of land, capital and labour

analyse the factors determining rent, interest and wages

distinguish between transfer earnings and economic rent.

Content

- Rent, interest, wages and profits
- Derived demand
  - The assumptions and limitations of marginal productivity theory
  - Marginal physical product, marginal revenue product and their relationship
- The value of the marginal product:
  - Land
  - Labour
  - Capital – using present value (use of graphical representation required)
- The fixity of land, the supply of loanable funds and the labour supply
- The demand for and supply of factors
- Numerical, graphical and verbal explanations of transfer earnings and economic rent

Introduction: factors of production

In economics there are four factors of production: land, labour, capital and entrepreneurship. Land is defined as all the natural resources that contribute to the production of goods and services, and includes resources such as wind and wave. Labour is defined as the human contribution, be it in the form of technical or physical expertise, to the production of goods and services, while capital refers to all man-made materials used in the production process. Entrepreneurship refers to the factor that combines all the other factors of production together to produce output.

The demand for these factors of production is referred to as derived demand, that is, it is directly linked to the demand for the final goods and services that they are used to produce. As such these factors of production or rather the owners of these factors of production earn income as a reward for participation in the production process. The reward to land is referred to as rent, to labour, wages, to capital, interest and to entrepreneurship, the return is profit.

Land: rent

The reward to the utilisation of land as a factor of production in the production mix is referred to as rent or economic rent. Land, as a factor of production, is often assumed to be fixed. However, constantly improving technologies have resulted in an expansion in the potential of this resource over time. For example, proven oil and gas reserves in Trinidad and Tobago have been increasing as a result of new exploration technologies. Table 8.1 on page 146 shows that the amount of reserves, both oil and gas, in Trinidad and Tobago increased between 1992 and 2004. No doubt finding the increase in reserves was due to improvements in the application of newer seismic technologies in the petrochemical sector.

Table 8.1 *Trinidad and Tobago reserves, 1992–2004*

Year	Crude oil reserves (m barrels)	Natural gas reserves (bn m³)
1992	573	238
1993	541	233
1994	488	230
1995	560	286
1996	565	349
1997	551	456
1998	584	517
1999	534	560
2000	605	603
2001	686	664
2002	716	558
2003	716	589
2004	990	650

Source: World Oil and Gas Review 2004

Labour: wages

The compensation to labour for its contribution to the production of goods and services is known as wages and salaries. A wage is the amount paid for a specific quantity of labour, for a particular task, while a salary is a form of periodic payment from the employer to the employee for ongoing work. Both wages and salaries are returns to labour effort.

Capital: interest

The return to capital is interest. The term 'capital' is used to describe both physical and financial investments in the production of goods and services, where the price of utilisation is referred to as the rental price of capital or interest.

Entrepreneur: profits

Entrepreneurs initiate businesses and develop clever ways of producing and distributing goods. They seize opportunities in the market by investing and taking risks. The entrepreneur is rewarded for this with profits.

The concept of derived demand

The demand for a factor of production is different from the demand for a final good. In particular, final goods are demanded for their own sake, while factors of production are demanded as an input into a production process. For example, the demand for land on which cocoa is grown is derived from the demand for cocoa. Alternatively, if there exists a demand for cocoa there will be a demand for the factors of production to produce cocoa.

Activity 8.1

What are the rewards associated with each of the four factors of production?

Feedback

The reward associated with land is rent, with labour it is wages, with capital it is interest and with entrepreneurship it is profits.

The theory of distribution

The theory of distribution focuses on providing an understanding of how factor markets clear. Just as the price mechanism works to determine the price of goods in the various market structures, price determination in factor markets works in a similar way to determine the returns to factors of production under varying assumptions about market competitiveness.

In the simple theory of distribution elaborated here, all factors of production are assumed to be owned by households. Households sell these factors of production to firms and receive factor incomes in return. Factor incomes (together with other influences on demand) working through the price mechanism provide an outlet for the consumption of final goods and services. The demand for final goods and services in turn leads to a derived demand for factor services, which again, working through the price mechanism, interact with the availability of factors of production to determine the extent of factor employment and their remuneration. This circular flow is shown in Figure 8.1 below.

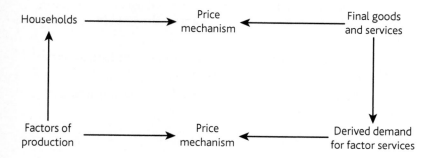

Figure 8.1 *The relationship between factor and commodity markets*

As with commodity markets, factor markets are characterised by different degrees of imperfection. As such, factor markets can range from being perfectly competitive to being monopolistic or even monopsonistic in nature. Monopolistic factor markets refer to those market situations where there is only one seller of the particular resource. One buyer, on the other hand, characterises monopsonistic factor markets.

The demand and supply conditions of various of factors of production

Land

The demand for land

To discuss the concept of the value of the marginal product of land, consider the following example of a cassava farmer who is considering renting land to plant cassava. How much land should they rent? Well that is easy, that will depend on the rent per acre of land or in other words the price of the land.

Using the general formula, the marginal productivity of land can be determined as

$$MP_{Land} = \frac{\Delta Output}{\Delta Land}$$

With the change in output being measured in pounds of cassava, the value of the marginal product (VMP) is determined as the product of price of the final output (cassava) and the marginal product of land. The VMP is therefore calculated using the following formula:

$$VMP_{Land} = p^{*}MP_{Land}$$

To the cassava farmer the value of the marginal productivity of land is the market value of the cassava produced on one additional acre of land. The farmer will therefore increase the amount of acres they rent until the following criterion is met:

$$VMP_{Land} = price_{Land}$$

As the market price for land falls, therefore, the farmer would have to increase their consumption of land in order to restore equilibrium conditions. The value of the marginal product of land curve therefore corresponds to the demand curve for land of a standard quality.

Supply of land

In general it is assumed that the supply of land is fixed although it can be argued that over time, as technology changes, the yield from a piece of land can improve.

Given the assumption of fixed land, the supply curve for land is vertical or perfectly inelastic or unresponsive to price changes.

The equilibrium market price for land is therefore determined by the demand for the factor. Figure 8.2 illustrates this.

Labour

Labour supply to the firm and industry

The market supply of a factor of production can be represented as:

$$MS_L = \Sigma IS_L$$

where MS_L is the market supply of labour and IS_L is the individual labour curves of all the workers in the industry. This implies that the market supply of labour or rather a particular type of labour is the sum total of the individual supply curves of each unit of labour or labour type.

When a worker supplies their labour to the market, the worker will derive utility. This utility has two main parts, (a) the utility from receiving an actual wage and (b) the utility from actually working.

While it is clear that one work can offer a different degree of utility as compared to another, we shall assume for the purpose of analysis that the utility from work is initially zero, so that the worker's net advantage from working, which is the sum of utility from work and utility from receiving a wage, is equivalent to the worker's utility from wages. In other words, for the purposes of analysis, the assumption made is that the only utility derived from work is the utility from wages earned.

If it is assumed that an individual can use their time either to work or engage in leisure activities, then it can be deduced that the worker's marginal utility from earning a wage is equivalent to the worker's marginal utility from leisure.

Figure 8.3 shows the supply curve of labour. Note that at a wage level below W_0, workers are not prepared to offer any labour effort on the market. It can be understood, therefore, that in order to entice more

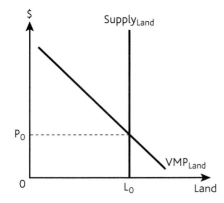

Figure 8.2 *Demand and supply curves for land*

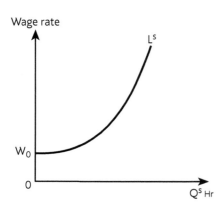

Figure 8.3 *Supply curve of labour*

work hours from workers, firms will have to offer progressively higher wage rates. This pattern results in an upward-sloping supply curve of labour.

Changes in supply of labour

The supply of labour changes, resulting in shifts of the supply curve when the size of the population changes or when technology and the capital base of an economy changes.

Marginal productivity theory: the demand curve for labour

Assumption of marginal revenue productivity theory

Marginal revenue productivity theory is based on two main assumptions, firstly that the product market is perfectly competitive, the implication of which is that marginal revenue remains constant, and secondly that the factor market is perfectly competitive.

In a perfectly competitive goods market, a firm can sell any amount of the commodity it produces at the prevailing market price. In a similar way, if a factor market is characterised by perfect competition, the firm can purchase any amount of a factor, for example labour, at the prevailing market wage rate. Thus, at the prevailing market wage rate, the marginal and average cost of employing factors of production is the same for the firm.

The marginal physical productivity of labour refers to the amount of additional output of a commodity that an extra worker produces.

Recall the law of diminishing marginal returns, which implies that as an increasing amount of a variable factor is utilised in conjunction with a given amount of a fixed factor, the returns to the variable factor eventually decrease. This is reflected in Figure 8.4, which shows output of each additional unit of labour, with the L_{0th} worker, the firm benefits by Q_0 units being added to total output, while with the L_{1st} worker the addition decreases to Q_1. The MPP of labour is calculated to show the change in output derived from hiring each additional unit of labour.

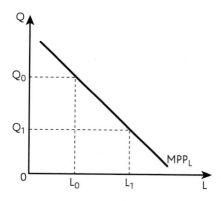

Figure 8.4 *Marginal physical product of labour*

To determine the value of the marginal physical product of the worker it is necessary to multiply the marginal physical product of each worker by the marginal revenue each unit of the output produced by the firm fetches. In Figure 8.5 below, the marginal revenue earned by the firm for each unit of output the worker produces is shown.

The marginal revenue product curve, which shows the revenue earned by each consecutive unit of labour hired, is based on the output produced by that unit of labour. Due to the law of diminishing returns the output produced by each unit of labour falls and as such the marginal revenue product of each unit of labour also falls. It follows therefore (and Figure 8.6 overleaf reflects this) that the firm will demand labour up to the point where the marginal revenue product (MPP × MR = MRP) generated by a particular worker is just equal to the wage rate the worker receives. In that if the worker is paid a rate above that which he generates for the firm then the firm absorbs this loss. On the other hand, if the wage rate paid is less than that which the worker generates for the firm, then there is the incentive for the individual worker to lower their level of productivity.

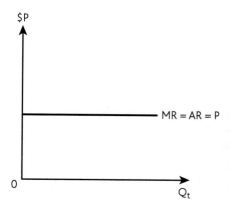

Figure 8.5 *Marginal revenue of labour*

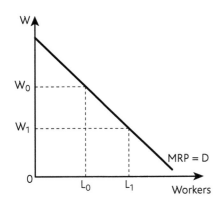

Figure 8.6 *The marginal revenue product curve*

A firm will therefore be willing to pay a wage rate that is equal to the level of revenue generated by that unit of labour.

The MRP curve is thus the demand curve for labour of the firm. At the wage rate of W_0 the firm will demand L_0 workers. If the wage rate falls to W_1 the number of workers employed would increase to L_1 workers. A firm would hire workers up to the point where the marginal revenue product of the last unit of labour is equal to the wage rate. As the wage rate falls, the firm is in disequilibrium where the wage rate is less than the marginal revenue product of the last unit of labour. As more labour is hired the marginal revenue product falls and equilibrium is restored.

Changes in the demand for labour

The demand curve for labour can shift when the price of final commodity prices change, the price of factors of production change or if technology changes.

Limitations of marginal revenue productivity theory

There are a number of well-known deficiencies with the marginal productivity theory of wage determination, including the following:

- In practice, it is very difficult if not impossible to determine the marginal physical productivity of service workers or administrative staff, as they do not directly produce a measurable output.

- The MRP theory assumes that the other factors of production are held constant while labour changes. In practice, many firms substitute capital for labour or change their capital stock as their labour force changes. If the inputs of the other factors of production change, then it will be very difficult to measure the MPP and MRP of labour accurately.

- The assumption of the freedom of entry into and exit from the labour market is not realistic. Labour markets today are characterised by a substantial amount of distortions in terms of the presence of trade unions and other types of informational asymmetries and market imperfections. One of the main imperfections of labour markets is that of labour immobility.

- Backward-bending labour supply curves. As wages increase, it is not always the case that there is an increase in the quantity supplied of labour. Specifically, economic theory reveals that as income increases above a particular threshold, the supply of labour actually falls. This is because individuals will begin to substitute more leisure for work beyond this point. This concept can be shown below using indifference curve analysis.

The individual's indifference curve in the context of Figure 8.7 shows the various combinations of leisure and income per day, which give workers the same level of satisfaction. The slope of the budget line is derived using the wage rate and leisure hours. Original consumer equilibrium occurs at point a. As the wage rate increases the budget line pivots outwards and consumer equilibrium now occurs at point b, which is to the right of a. At this point the individual substitutes the leisure time for work as the return increases.

The budget line pivots further outward and, as the income increases, the new consumer equilibrium is to the left of b, shown by the point c. In this case the individual substitutes working hours for leisure. This may be due to the fact that they may be able to work fewer hours and still maintain the same standard of living, complemented by more leisure time. This type of behaviour results in the backward bend of the supply curve for labour.

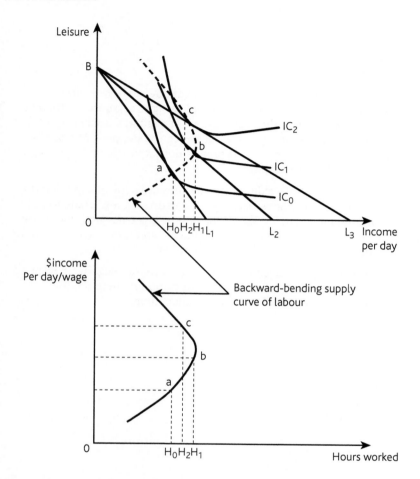

Figure 8.7 *The backward-bending supply curve*

Capital

Demand for capital

Capital refers to the man-made contributions to the production of goods and services. The firm will demand capital up to the point where the marginal revenue product of capital is exactly equal to the price of capital. However, consider that the returns to capital accrue over time as compared to the cost of capital, which has to be undertaken in the current period. As such, in order to evaluate the true value of the return to capital the marginal revenue product must be discounted to determine its present value.

Discounting refers to the process of converting a future amount of finances into a current period valuation. The present value of future resources is the amount that, if invested today, it will yield if the market interest rate is taken into account.

To determine the present value of future income the following formula is used:

$$PV = FV/(1 + r)^t$$

where

PV: present value

FV: future value

r: interest rate

t: time in years.

The net present value is calculated as the difference between the discounted marginal revenue product and the cost of capital. If the net present value is positive, then investment in capital is feasible and the firm should purchase the capital. If, however, the net present value is negative then the investment in capital is not profitable and the firm should not purchase the capital.

A rise in the interest rate reduces the net present value of capital and, as such, as the interest rates rise, fewer investment projects are found to be feasible and hence undertaken. The opposite is true such that as the interest rate declines the net present value of capital increases and more projects become feasible and hence undertaken.

The quantity of capital investment projects therefore negatively responds to the interest rate. The demand curve for capital is therefore the downward-sloping marginal revenue product curve.

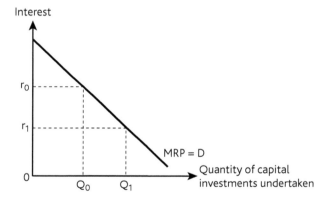

Figure 8.8 *The marginal revenue product curve for capital*

Supply of capital

The quantity of capital supplied to the market is dependent on people's saving patterns, decisions and behaviour. Some of the main factors that determine the level of savings include income levels, expected future income levels and the going interest rate.

The supply curve of resources available for capital investment shows the relationship between the interest rate and the quantity of capital resources supplied, *ceteris paribus*. A rise in the interest rate results in an increase in the amount of capital brought to the market and a movement along the savings supply curve.

The savings supply curve, also known as the loanable funds curve, shifts if the size and age distribution of the population changes or if the level of income changes. The equilibrium interest rate is determined by the interaction of the demand for and supply of capital.

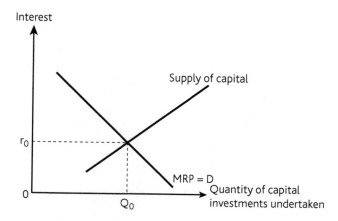

Figure 8.9 *Equilibrium interest rate*

Economic rent and transfer earnings

The early theory of economic rent (ER) was initially developed in relation to land, but it is now widely understood that the term 'economic rent' refers to any payment to a factor of production above the minimum it would be willing to take in order to keep it in its current deployment. Transfer earnings (TE) refer to the minimum amount that the factor requires to stay in its current post. Consider Figure 8.10.

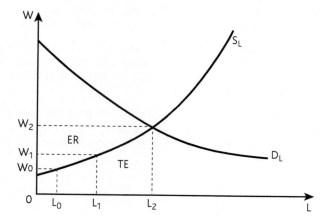

Figure 8.10 *Transfer earnings and economic rent*

The total earnings of these L_2 workers is W_2L_2. Observe that L_0 workers, however, are willing to work for an average wage of W_0, while L_1 workers are willing to work for W_1. Let us now consider these L_0 workers in greater detail. Each of these L_0 workers was willing to supply their services for $\$W_0$ but are now receiving $\$W_2$. The difference $W_2 - W_0$ represents the economic rent of these workers and $\$W_0$ represents their transfer earnings.

A number of permutations between economic rent and transfer earnings can therefore be cast in the following manner.

Example

A teacher earning $10,000 a month gives up their job and takes unskilled work at $7,000 per month. In this case, the transfer earnings are $7,000 while the economic rent is $3,000. A famous pop star earning $50,000 a month falls in popularity and takes a job that pays $10,000 a month. In this case their economic rent is $40,000. It can therefore be concluded that the scarcer the supply of a factor (e.g. a particular type of labour), the greater the economic rent is likely to be. Economic rent therefore is equal to the portion of income earned that is above that of transfer earnings.

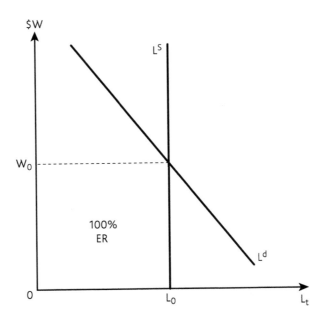

Figure 8.11 *Economic rent under perfectly inelastic supply of labour*

In Figure 8.11 the vertical perfectly inelastic supply curve of labour indicates that at a wage rate of $0 L_0 workers will still be supplied to the market. In the event that these L_0 workers receive $$W_0$ then they may obtain an economic rent of W_0L_0, that is, all of their earnings are economic rent.

In another permutation (Figure 8.12), workers are only willing to supply their skills at a wage rate of $$W_1$ or nothing, that is, the supply of labour is perfectly elastic at this wage rate. In this case, the entire earnings of the workforce amount to transfer earnings.

In Figure 8.12 the factor is abundant in supply, for example the supply of teachers. As such, there is no need to pay the factor anything above its minimum earnings. Thus, the factor primarily earns transfer earnings.

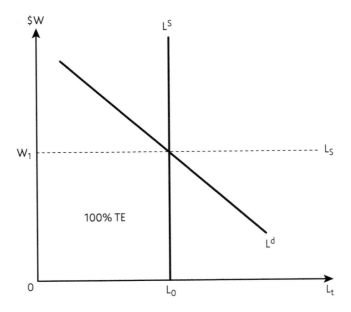

Figure 8.12 *Transfer earnings under relatively abundant factor supply*

Conclusion

This chapter reviewed the concepts of derived demand and proposed discussions regarding the rewards to the various factors of production. The theory of marginal productivity was applied to the demand for the various factors of production, land, labour and capital.

The factors affecting the supply of land, labour and capital were also dealt with. Discussions also included factors affecting transfer earnings and rent.

Key points

■ The demand for factors of production is referred to as derived demand, that is, it is directly linked to the demand for the final goods and services that they are used to produce. As such, these factors of production or rather the owners of these factors of production earn income as a reward for participation in the production process. The reward to land is referred to as rent, to labour it is wages, to capital it is interest and to entrepreneurship the return is profit.

■ The theory of distribution focuses on providing an understanding of how factor markets clear.

■ Marginal revenue productivity theory is based on two main assumptions, in particular that the product market is perfectly competitive, the implication of which is that marginal revenue remains constant and, secondly, that the factor market is perfectly competitive.

■ The term 'economic rent' refers to any payment to a factor of production above the minimum it would be willing to take in order to keep it in its current deployment.

■ Transfer earnings refer to the minimum amount that the factor requires to stay in its current post.

9 Wage differentials

Specific objectives

You should be able to:

explain the concept of wage differentials

analyse imperfections in the labour market

analyse the effect of labour mobility on wages

explain the concept of compensating wage differentials

explain the role of government, trade unions and employers' associations in the pricing of labour.

Content

- Differences in wages within industries and among industries
- Imperfections on the demand side (e.g. differences in marginal productivity) and on the supply side (e.g. geographical immobility)

Wage differentials

Wage differentials can be defined as the difference in wage rates between two classes of workers. Wage differentials can be attributed to a host of factors including differences in skills and formal qualifications, experience and training, whether or not labour is unionised, and the age of workers. Consider that wage differentials can exist in the teaching profession. For example, it is conceivable that a teacher with 25 years' experience would receive a different salary level as compared to a teacher with two years' teaching experience.

Wage differentials can therefore occur within particular industries and also across industries. For example, in the food service industry different kinds of workers would receive a different salary level. Consider the average restaurant that employs bartenders, hostesses, servers, busers, kitchen workers and delivery workers. In Ontario, for example, the established wage policy indicates that:

> If an employee serves liquor as a regular part of their employment, regardless of the length of time during the shift they actually serve liquor directly to patrons, they will be considered to be entitled to the liquor servers' minimum wage for all hours worked during the shift. (Canadian Restaurant and Foodservices Association (2008) Minimum Wage and Differentials – Targeted Relief to a Hard Hit Industry, from www.crfa.ca)

Factors affecting wage differentials

- Education and training: in general, individuals who are formally educated and trained will tend to command higher salaries. The cost of further education will be less than the income in the future. These individuals increase their earning potential by gaining skills and knowledge. Hence carpenters and masons will be paid more than a labourer on construction sites and doctors will command a higher salary than bus drivers.

- Age and experience: younger workers will earn lower salaries than those who are older and have more experience. When young persons enter the labour market they often do not have the practical know-how of the more experienced workers and as such will be eligible for a lower salary.

Example

Wage differentials and teaching in Barbados

Teachers in Barbados are paid according to the salary scales set out by the government. These scales are as follows.

Scale	Post	Range (BDS$)
S4	Principal	109,114.44
S6	Deputy Principal	88,182.96
Z 15–Z 2	Trained Graduate	44,950.80 to 66,192.72
Z 15–Z 5	Untrained Graduate	44,950.80 to 60,348.72
Z 22–Z 28	Trained Non-Graduate	37,642.80 to 55,339.08
Z 22–Z 6	Special Grade	37,642.80 to 58,586.76
Z 36–Z 24	Untrained Non-Graduate	24,980.04 to 35,646.48

The top two posts are management positions and will require not only experience but a certificate in education. The untrained non-graduate will not have the qualifications or the experience to function in such a post.

■ Demand and supply conditions: wage rates will tend to be higher in labour markets where demand is high and inelastic or where supply is low and inelastic (e.g. specialty surgeons) than in markets where demand is low and elastic or where supply is high and elastic (see Figure 9.1 below).

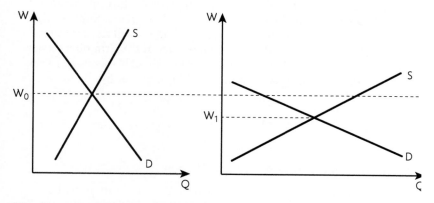

Figure 9.1 *Demand and supply conditions for labour and its impact on wages*

Wage determination under conditions of perfect competition

In Figure 9.2 on page 158, the perfectly competitive labour market is in equilibrium with a wage rate of W^*, employing L^* workers, where market supply is equal to market demand for labour. At any wage rate above equilibrium, such as W_1, the supply of labour is greater than the demand. There will be a surplus of labour on the market, which will drive the wage rate downward to W^*. On the other hand, at any wage rate below equilibrium, such as at W_2, the demand for labour is greater than supply labour. A shortage of labour will be created, which will serve to push wages upward to W^*.

At the market equilibrium wage rate of W*, the individual firm hires L_1 units of labour.

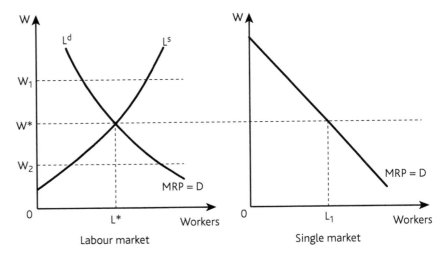

Figure 9.2 *Market equilibrium*

Wage determination under conditions of imperfect competition

If it is assumed that in a particular labour market only a single firm hires, then demand in this market is referred to as being monopsonistic. A monopsony situation occurs when there is only one buyer of a commodity or service. In a monopsonistic environment, workers enter the market more easily as the wage rate improves. Thus, in Figure 9.2 at a wage rate of W_0 the firm will employ say L_0 workers. Suppose the firm decides it requires L_1 (L_0 + 1) workers, then it will need to offer a higher wage rate to attract the marginal worker. If the firm offers a new wage W_1 to the new worker it is also obligated to offer this wage to the other L_0 workers so that the overall wage bill increases by:

$$= (L_0 + 1) \, W_1 = L_0 W_0$$
$$= W_1 L_0 + W_1 - L_0 W_0$$
$$= L_0 \, (W_1 - W_0) + W_1$$

This is clearly more than W_1 as $W_1 - W_0 > 0$.

Under conditions of imperfect competition, the wage rate must be increased to attract each extra unit of labour. In addition to this, the firm will also have to pay this higher wage rate to each of the labour units hired previously so that the firm's wage bill increases as more units of labour are hired.

In this regard then we can draw the firm's average input cost (AIC) and marginal input cost (MIC) curves for a firm. Where the marginal input cost refers to the total increase in the firm's wage bill as a result of hiring one more unit of labour, the average input cost is the average wage paid to each unit of labour employed.

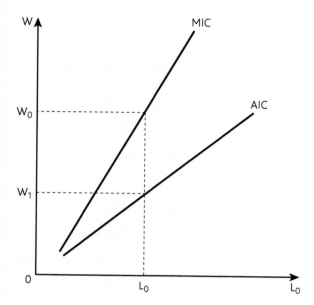

Figure 9.3 *Average input cost and marginal input cost*

The mobility of labour

Varying market conditions of demand and supply for labour result in a situation where wage levels differ across markets. For instance, in a situation where the demand for labour is relatively high as compared to supply the market wage rate would be higher than if the demand for labour was low relative to supply. The wage rate would also be higher if the supply of labour was relatively less than the demand for labour, as compared to a situation where the supply of labour was relatively higher than demand.

In situations where wage levels vary because of the differences in the market demand and supply conditions for labour, labour would tend to move out of markets where the wage rate is low and into markets where wage rates are higher. As a consequence, in low-wage markets the supply of labour would fall and over time wages would rise. In high-wage markets, the supply of labour would increase and over time wage rates would fall. In these cases, the mobility of labour has resulted in the convergence of wages in different markets. Labour mobility in this context is defined as the ability of labour to move between industries, sectors and jobs.

In reality, labour may not be able to move easily between markets. This is a case of labour immobility. If this immobility persists in the long run then wages between markets would not converge.

There are two types of labour mobility, geographical mobility and occupational mobility. Geographical mobility relates to moving between similar jobs that are located in two different geographical places. An example of geographical mobility is moving from Trinidad to Barbados as a nurse. Geographical immobility therefore implies that labour is unable to move between geographical areas to take up job opportunities.

Occupational mobility is concerned with workers switching between sectors. An example of occupational mobility is a teacher becoming an accountant. Occupational immobility therefore implies that labour cannot easily move between sectors.

Activity 9.1

A firm currently employs 10 workers at a cost of $100 per day. If it hires an eleventh worker, then it has to pay each worker $110 per day. Calculate the average and marginal cost of hiring the eleventh worker.

Feedback

A firm currently employs 10 workers at $100 each per day. Assume that the firm desires to increase employment from 10 workers to 11 workers. This necessitates that it offers $110 to the eleventh worker. Because union regulations will require that the first 10 workers also receive $110 per hour the firm's wage bill therefore increases as follows:

Cost of employing
10 workers at
$100 each   = $1,000

Cost of employing
11 workers at
$110 each   = $1,210

Average cost
of employing
11 workers   = $110

Marginal cost
of employing the
eleventh worker = $1,210 − 1,000

                 = $210

Clearly $210 > $110, indicating that the marginal cost of employing the eleventh worker is more than the average cost of employing the 11 workers.

Compensating (equalising) differentials

Compensating or equalising differentials refers to the bonus paid to certain types of labour for 'undesirable work'. Alternatively it refers to the additional amount of money paid for a job that has negative externalities. For example, consider the job of a nurse. A nurse is exposed to various health hazards in the work place and, as such, besides a salary to which the nurse is entitled, they may also have access to guaranteed government housing and a travelling and insurance allowance that can be considered as a compensating differential for undertaking the risk associated with their profession.

The role of government in wage determination

The government may intervene in the labour market to determine wage levels via minimum wage legislation, for example. A minimum wage is a legally enforced benchmark price of labour, often quoted per hour. Minimum wage legislation is aimed at ensuring that workers achieve and maintain a decent standard of living and have access to basic goods and services.

The role of trade unions in wage determination

Trade unions can influence wages via collective bargaining. Collective bargaining refers to the process by which workers unite to negotiate wages and other working conditions with employers. Collective bargaining lends strength to workers' concerns but can also contribute to inefficiency in the market, such that if trade unions lobby for a wage level represented by W_u then the demand for labour would increase from Q_0 to Q_1 (see Figure 9.4). In this case the union was successful in increasing both the level of employment and the wage rate in this market.

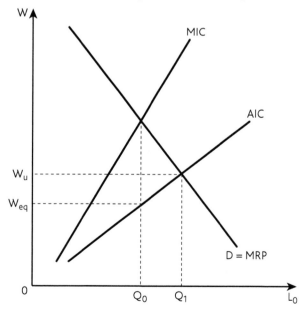

Figure 9.4 *Wage determination (1)*

If the trade union lobbies for a wage level represented by $W_u{}^*$, the demand for labour may decrease from $Q_0{}^*$ to $Q_1{}^*$ (see Figure 9.5). In this situation, although the wage rate increases, the level of employment in the market falls.

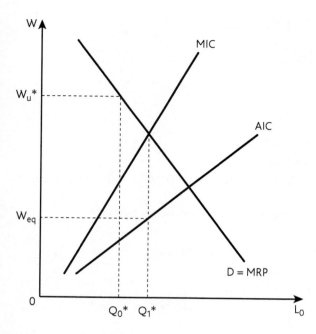

Figure 9.5 *Wage determination (2)*

Conclusion

This chapter considered the concept of wage differentials. The various factors resulting in labour market imperfections were also analysed. The impact of labour mobility on wages was also illustrated and the concept of compensating wage differentials was introduced.

The role of the government, trade unions and employers' associations in wage determination was also discussed.

Key points

- Wage differentials can be defined as the difference in wage rates between two classes of workers.
- Wage differentials can be attributed to a host of factors including differences in skills and formal qualifications, experience and training, whether or not labour is unionised, and the age of workers; consider that wage differentials can exist in the teaching profession.
- Compensating or equalising differentials refer to the bonus paid to certain types of labour for 'undesirable work'. Alternatively, it refers to the additional amount of money paid for a job that has negative externalities.

10 Income inequality, poverty and poverty alleviation

Specific objectives

You should be able to:

differentiate between size and functional distribution of income

explain the concept of income inequality

explain the measures of income inequality

explain the measures used to reduce income inequality

distinguish between absolute and relative poverty

outline factors that contribute to poverty

explain why certain categories of people are more susceptible to poverty than others

evaluate the different ways used to measure poverty

outline strategies used by governments to alleviate poverty

analyse the economic costs of poverty

assess the economic benefits of government intervention to alleviate poverty.

Content

- Size and functional distribution of income
- How income is distributed
- Lorenz curve measurement of income inequality; and Gini coefficient (interpretation only)
- Measures to reduce inequality: taxes, subsidies, transfers
- Absolute versus relative poverty
- Factors that contribute to poverty including:
  - Social and physical environment
  - Discrimination – gender, race
  - Restrictions on certain economic activities
  - Non-ownership of resources
  - Family size
  - Single parent; female-headed families
- Persons who are most susceptible to poverty:
  - People with special needs:
    - Physically challenged
    - Elderly
    - Youth
    - Single-parent families
    - Indigenous people
  - Reasons – limited access to employment, level of training, legislation, availability of income to share among family
- Ways used to measure poverty:
  - Basic needs
  - Poverty line
  - Head count
  - UNDP Human Development Index (HDI)
- Strategies to alleviate poverty:
  - Transfer payments
  - Free education and health care
  - Housing
  - Minimum wage legislation
  - Equal employment opportunities
  - Government employment creation (special works programmes)
- The cost of poverty, including:
  - Unemployed human resources
  - Lower potential output
  - Inefficient allocation of government expenditure
  - Social and environmental costs

■ Economic benefits including:

    ■ Provision of education and health leading to development of human capital

    ■ Improvement in well-being as measured by the UNDP HDI

    ■ More equitable distribution of income

The size and functional distribution of income

The size distribution of income refers to the distribution of income by individuals, families and households. In other words, it relates to income distribution among economic agents. The size distribution of income is the most common form of measuring income distribution.

The functional distribution of income or the factor share of income distribution refers to the distribution of income between the various factors of production. The theory is concerned with measuring the share of wages, as compared to interest, wages and profits.

We can illustrate the functional distribution of income with reference to Figure 10.1 below. Assuming that there are only two factors of production: capital (a fixed factor of production) and labour (a variable factor).

The assumption is made of perfect competition and, as such, the demand for labour is dependent on the marginal productivity of labour, also the traditional neoclassical supply curve is upward sloping and shown as S_L.

Figure 10.1 shows that, given the conditions, the equilibrium wage rate is W_0 with E_0 employed. The level of national output produced will be represented by the area $0REE_0$. This total output is distributed as area $0W_0EE_0$, allocated to labour in the form of wages, and W_0RE, being distributed as profits among the owners of capital.

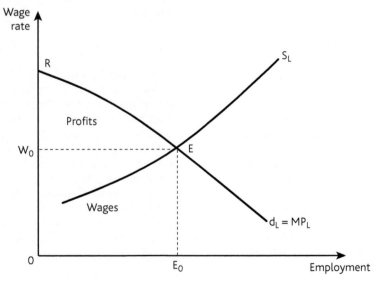

Figure 10.1 *The functional distribution of income*

Although the functional distribution of income theory does provide the framework within which the perfectly competitive labour market can be analysed, its relevance in modern-day economics is diminished due to the fact that it does not consider the non-market forces that influence wage rates, such as collective bargaining and unionisation.

The concept of income inequality

The concept of inequality relates to the maldistribution of income across economic agents or across sectors.

Measurement of inequality

The Lorenz curve

The Lorenz curve was developed in 1905 by Max Lorenz to measure the extent of inequality in the distribution of income. We can illustrate the Lorenz curve by making reference to Figure 10.2 below.

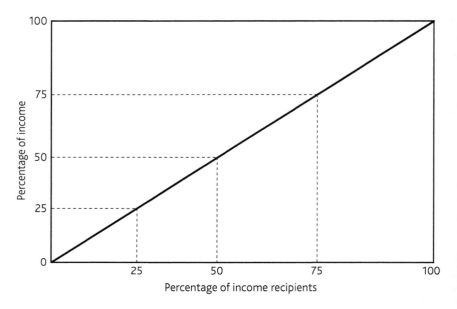

Figure 10.2 *The Lorenz curve (an egalitarian economy)*

The horizontal axis shows the number of income recipients in the economy in cumulative percentage terms. As such, the point 50 on the diagram represents 50 per cent of total income recipients, while the point 75 represents 75 per cent of total income recipients. On the vertical axis the percentage of income is shown. Thus the point 25 represents 25 per cent of total income. If the economy is an egalitarian income-earning society where everyone earns the same wage, then the first 25 per cent of income earners will account for 25 per cent of the total income, 50 per cent of income recipients would earn 50 per cent of total income and so on. In this type of society a diagonal line such as that drawn in the diagram above will characterise the distribution of income and will reflect that the percentage of income recipients will be identical to the share of total income earned by labour.

This diagonal line therefore provides an exact relationship between each successive income recipient and the share of income accounted for by labour.

The Lorenz curve shows the actual distribution of income in an economy. In particular, it shows the share of income earned by varying amounts of income recipients.

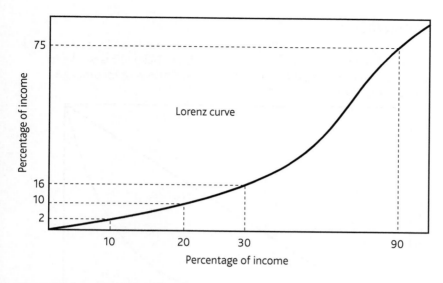

Figure 10.3 *Derivation of the Lorenz curve*

To explain the Lorenz curve some hypothetical data is used: 10 per cent of income recipients receive 2 per cent of total income, while 20 per cent of all income earners receive 10 per cent of all income. Observe that, as constructed, 90 per cent of the income earners earn only 75 per cent of all income, implying that the richest 10 per cent of the population earns 25 per cent of all income.

The Lorenz curve can adopt a variety of shapes as illustrated in the diagram below.

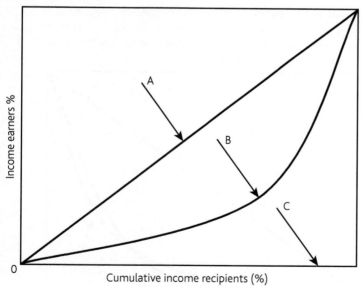

Figure 10.4 *Varying shapes of the Lorenz curve*

There are three Lorenz curves in Figure 10.4. Lorenz curve A shows perfect equality in the distribution of income amongst all income earners, while Lorenz curve C shows perfect inequality, which shows that 99 per cent of the income earners earn 0 per cent of income and the top 1 per cent of income earners earn all the income. Thus, the further away from the line of equality the Lorenz curve lies, the greater the quantum of income inequality in the economy.

Gini coefficient

The Gini coefficient is another measure of inequality and was developed by the Italian statistician Corrado Gini, who published his works in 1912. The index is used to measure the distribution of income, and ranges from 0 to 1.

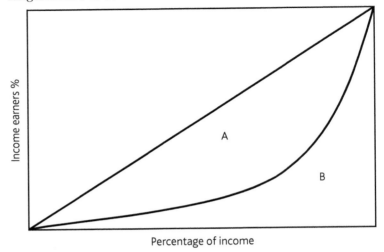

Figure 10.5 *Deriving the Gini coefficient from the Lorenz curve*

The Gini coefficient can be represented as the ratio of area A to A and B, that is,

$$\text{Gini} = {}^{A}/_{A+B}$$

The Gini coefficient is useful when Lorenz curves intersect such as in Figure 10.6. A value that tends to 1 indicates that the level of income inequality is higher, while a lower level of inequality is represented by a Gini coefficient that tends towards 0.

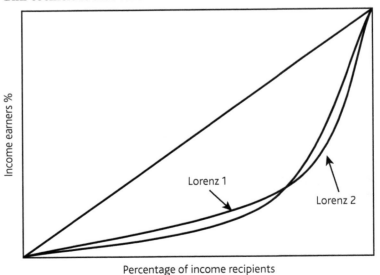

Figure 10.6 *Intersecting Lorenz curves*

Consider Table 10.1, which shows the Gini coefficient for the OECS countries. It can be concluded therefore that among this grouping, Antigua and Barbuda had the most uneven distribution of income and St Kitts and Nevis the most even.

Table 10.1 *Gini coefficients for OECS, 1995*

Antigua – Barbuda	0.525
Dominica	0.488
Grenada	0.504
St Kitts – Nevis	0.445
St Vincent	0.448
St Lucia	0.468

Source: http://www.sdnp.org.gy

Activity 10.1

Discuss some measures to reduce the degree of income inequality existing in an economy.

Measures to reduce income inequality

Taxes

Progressive taxes can be used to reduce the extent of income inequality in a society. Progressive taxation systems place a larger tax burden, in terms of proportion of income, on higher tax brackets than lower tax brackets. For example, persons earning less than $60,000 a year bear the burden of 5 per cent income in income tax, while persons earning between $60,000 and $150,000 per year bear the burden on 15 per cent income tax.

Subsidies

Subsidies can also be used to supplement income inequality in that such facilities can be used to increase the effective access of the poor and vulnerable in society to goods and services that improve standards of living. For example, an education subsidy such as the Dollar for Dollar (DfD) and Getting Access to Tertiary Education (GATE) programmes offered to undergraduate students in Trinidad and Tobago. In particular these subsidies enable those persons in society who would not have been able to access tertiary-level education because they lacked the financial resources to do so. Consider Table 10.2 below. Note that the DfD programme started in 2000/01 and offered students 50 per cent tuition coverage. GATE was started in 2003/04 and offered students 100 per cent coverage of tuition fees. Note that in 2000/01 total enrolment was approximately 10 per cent more than in 1997/98. In 2003/04 total enrolment was 60 per cent higher than in 1997/98 and some 46 per cent higher than in 2000/01.

Table 10.2 *Student enrolment at UWI St Augustine Campus by programme and faculty, 1997/98–2003/04*

Programme	1997/98	1998/99	1999/2000	2000/01	2001/02	2002/03	2003/04
First degrees	3,863	4,072	4,245	4,342	4,743	6,003	6,566
Certificate/diplomas	477	513	421	388	433	477	469
Higher degrees/advanced diplomas	1,982	2,075	2,190	2,194	2,424	2,177	3,087
Total	6,322	6,660	6,856	6,924	7,600	8,657	10,122
Faculty	**1997/98**	**1998/99**	**1999/2000**	**2000/01**	**2001/02**	**2002/03**	**2003/04**
Engineering	1,168	1,222	1,276	1,293	1,388	1,566	1,880
Humanities and education	1,347	1,458	1,571	1,577	1,688	1,796	2,101
Law	38	37	43	37	45	51	60
Medical sciences	832	925	968	947	1,004	1,059	1,103
Science and agriculture	1,313	1,388	1,339	1,292	1,434	1,669	2,189
Social sciences	1,624	1,630	1,659	1,778	2,141	2,516	2,789
Total	6,322	6,660	6,856	6,924	7,600	8,657	10,122

Source: CSO Annual Statistical Digest (various years)

Subsidies also exist for primary health care, basic foodstuffs and utilities.

Transfers

A transfer or transfer payment refers to payments aimed towards reducing the extent of the income inequality in society. Transfers are targeted at vulnerable groups in society, including the disabled, widows and orphans. Welfare payments can be considered as transfers.

Absolute and relative poverty

Poverty refers to the condition of persons who lack adequate levels of income and wealth to access basic human needs, such as access to clean water, health care, nutrition, shelter and clothing. People can be described as being absolutely or relatively poor. People are in a state of absolute poverty when the minimum basic human needs absorb all of their income. People can be described as relatively poor when the level of expenditure required to achieve an average standard of living is greater than their income levels.

Factors that contribute to poverty

There are a host of socio-economic, environmental and even political factors that contribute to poverty. Some of these are discussed below.

Social and physical environment

A person's social and physical environment relates to the conditions under which they live and work, their income levels and their educational background. These factors compound to either motivate a person to break free of the 'cycle of poverty' or to accept their current conditions as their long-run realities.

Discrimination

Discrimination is a factor that compounds the problem of poverty. Discrimination can occur on any basis, including gender, race, religion, marital status, income level or geography. Discrimination, especially in the workplace, may prevent persons from maximising their earning potential and as a consequence they remain in poverty.

Restrictions to certain economic activities

Restrictions in terms of access to certain job opportunities may be the direct result of discrimination. Individuals without adequate education and skills will only have access to a limited range of low-paying jobs.

Non-ownership of resources

Owners of factors of production earn factor incomes. Owners of land earn rent when land is used to produce goods and services. Owners of capital earn interest, labour earns wages and entrepreneurs earn profits. Persons in poverty do not generally own factors of production other than their own skill, training and experience (labour) and as such the only income that can accrue to them is wages when they are employed on the labour market.

Family size

If household income is shared among members of a large family, then the average income per member of that family would be less than if the family had fewer members. In other words, the distribution of household income among family members can affect individual levels of expenditure and hence promote their impoverishment. This situation can be compounded if there is only one breadwinner or if the home is headed by a single parent.

Groups most vulnerable to poverty

There are several groups in society that are more vulnerable to poverty than others. These groups include the following:

■ Physically challenged. Physically challenged people often find difficulty in obtaining jobs which are facilitative of their special needs. As a consequence, this group may not easily obtain employment and may remain in poverty.

■ Older persons. The elderly by definition are not of working age. Unless they have an adequate pension, investments or family support, they will live in poverty.

■ Young people. Youths in any society may also be susceptible to poverty. In the first instance, youths entering the labour market may not possess the skills, training or experience needed by firms and as a consequence take a longer time to become gainfully employed.

■ Single-parent families. The average income earned by single-parent families is typically less than that of the average family unit that has two parents, other things constant. As a consequence such families may be more susceptible to poverty.

■ Indigenous peoples. As alluded to above, discrimination is a contributory factor in poverty. Indigenous peoples are often discriminated against in the workplace and as a consequence may not have access to the job opportunities that would allow them to improve their earning potential.

■ Illegal migrants. Illegal migrants tend to take low-paying jobs because they fear deportation. Children of illegal migrants will also not have access to education or basic health care because their parents cannot afford to pay for these services. As a consequence, the rate of poverty tends to be high among this portion of the population.

Measures of poverty

The extent of poverty in an economy can be measured using various indices. These include the following.

Basic needs

The basic needs approach is one of the primary ways of evaluating absolute poverty. The basic needs approach aims at defining the minimum amount of resources necessary for long-term physical well-being and determines the amount of expenditure necessary to achieve this. Some of the immediate basic needs included in this method are food, water, shelter and clothing. The basic needs poverty line defines the level of income required to achieve these needs.

Poverty line

A poverty line refers to the minimum level of income necessary to achieve a decent standard of living. There are absolute poverty lines, such as the basic needs poverty line, and there are relative poverty lines. A relative poverty line is generally a given percentage of the average income level. As such, relative poverty lines vary across economies and income levels.

Headcount

The headcount index of poverty is a measure of the prevalence of poverty and is calculated as the relative portion of the population that earns less than the defined poverty line. An increase in the headcount index implies a worsening of the poverty situation, as a larger proportion of the population is now defined as being poor.

The UNDP's Human Development Index

The Human Development Index (HDI) is a summary measure of the average achievement in a country founded on three dimensions of human development:

- Life expectancy at birth
- Knowledge, defined as a combination of the adult literacy rate (two-thirds weight) and the combined primary, secondary and tertiary level gross enrolment ratios (one third)
- An indication of the standard of living measured by GDP per capita (measured in Purchasing Power Parity (PPP) terms)

To calculate the overall HDI, the UNDP forms indices for each of these dimensions.

In each of these three dimensions, the performance of a country is evaluated as:

$$\text{Dimension index} = \frac{AV - Min\ V}{Max\ V - Min\ V}$$

where

AV: Average value

Min V: Minimum value

Max V: Maximum value

After each of these three-dimension indices are calculated, the overall HDI is calculated as the simple arithmetical average of all three.

Thus if

LE: Life expectancy index

E: Education index and

S: Standard of living index

Then

$$HDI = \frac{LE + E + S}{3}$$

HDI scores for several Caribbean countries

Table 10.3 *HDI scores for several Caribbean countries*

	1975	1980	1985	1990	2000	2002
Trinidad and Tobago	0.735	0.768	0.786	0.791	0.806	0.801
Barbados	0.804	0.827	0.837	0.851	0.888	0.888
Jamaica	0.687	0.695	0.699	0.726	0.752	0.764
Guyana	0.677	0.683	0.679	0.697	0.724	0.790
St Lucia	na	na	na	na	na	0.777
St Kitts	na	na	na	na	na	0.844
St Vincent	na	na	na	na	na	0.751
Suriname	na	na	na	na	na	0.780

Source: HDR 2000, 2004

From Table 10.3 on the previous page, in 2002 Barbados had the highest level of human development while St Vincent had the lowest level.

Measures to alleviate poverty

There are a number of measures that a country can implement in order to reduce the level of poverty. These policy measures can include:

- promote sustainable growth in a labour-intensive fashion
- increase the productivity of the poor by improving incentives to produce
- improve the safety nets to better target the needy
- implement policies that are geared towards improving the overall standard of living among the poor in a sustainable manner such as investment in primary health care and tertiary education.

Increasing the productivity of the poor involves:

- better training and education opportunities (at all stages of educational ladders)
- improving irrigation
- facilitating microfinance and micro-enterprise development.

Reducing poverty through economic growth

Economic growth in any economy is dependent on prudent fiscal and monetary policy, competition and optimal allocation of scarce resources. Trade liberalisation, including exchange rate liberalisation, is also critical to help foster the competitiveness of domestic exports in foreign markets.

In CARICOM economies where the capital stock is low, economic growth performance should have some degree of labour-intensive focus. Capital should not be excessively subsidised because this will create fiscal deficits.

Governments should also maintain exchange rates that are not overvalued.

Productivity of the poor

A critical strategy for overcoming poverty is to break the cycle of poverty by improving the productivity of the poor. The productivity of the poor can be increased by investing in their training and re-training at all levels of the development ladder. Not only must the productivity of the poor be improved but it must also be maintained. What we need to be able to do is to invest in health care so that the productivity of the poor can be improved and preserved.

Safety nets

Special programmes with a stipend helping unemployable people to re-enter the workplace should be engaged.

Transfer payments

Transfer payments can be used to alleviate poverty by augmenting the income levels of the vulnerable groups in society. This can ultimately positively impact their access to goods and services thereby improving their standard of living. In some countries the welfare department not only provides income for individuals, but it also provides food vouchers, pays utility bills, assists with rental accommodation and expenses and even assists persons who are HIV positive.

Free education and health care

Education and health care are merit goods. Poor people often do not have access to adequate educational opportunities or health-care benefits. Governments can provide these services free via subsidies in order to improve access of the poor to such goods. This has the direct impact of improving their standard of living. 'Free education' covers not only primary and secondary levels but also pre-primary and tertiary levels. Health care includes not only services provided by general hospitals and polyclinics, but also geriatrics and psychiatric care. The standard of living of the general population would increase especially for the 'at risk' groups like the elderly and the mentally ill.

Housing

The poor and vulnerable in society often do not have access to adequate housing with proper sanitation amenities. The provision of low-cost housing in this regard can enable the poor to improve their standard of living. For example, the Barbados government through the National Housing Corporation provides low-cost rental housing on a number of estates to enable the poor and other socially disadvantaged groups to have access to an adequate standard of living.

Minimum wage legislation

The enforcement of minimum wage legislation benefits the poor by improving income potential. One of the main aims of the imposition of a minimum wage is to ensure a decent standard of living for the most vulnerable group of workers in an economy.

Equal employment opportunities

Equal employment opportunities enable the poor to fill job vacancies that they are qualified for. In this regard equal employment opportunity rights help to address the problem of discrimination in the workplace.

Government employment creation

Government may also actively engage temporary employment schemes aimed at reducing poverty levels. Key examples of such programmes include the Unemployment Relief Program (URP) and the Community-Based Environmental Protection and Enhancement Program (CEPEP) administered by the Government of Trinidad and Tobago.

The economic benefits of poverty alleviation interventions

Several benefits accrue as a result of such interventions to reduce and alleviate poverty. In particular, where interventions include free education and health care, the long-run impact would be an improvement in the stock of human capital in an economy. Increased access to education enables the poor to improve their academic qualifications and access better job opportunities thereby breaking the cycle of poverty.

Improved access to health care has similar results, such that healthier people are more willing and better able to engage in productive activities and earn income to improve their standard of living.

Over time, as people become more productive, the level of poverty is expected to decline and the distribution of incomes will improve. These benefits will improve the long-run standard of living for an economy as a whole and also result in improvements in indicators, such as the HDI.

The economic costs of poverty

The existence of poverty in any economy has several negative implications on long-run economic growth. In particular some of the economic costs of poverty include the following.

Unemployed human resources

Poverty often occurs because of unemployment or underemployment. Unemployed resources have a negative long-run impact on an economy's growth potential. Recall the concept of economic inefficiency as illustrated by the production possibility curve in Chapter 1. Economic inefficiency is associated with production combinations within the production possibility frontier (PPF), the consequence of which is that national output would be lower than the potential level where all factors of production are employed. This situation is illustrated in Figure 10.7.

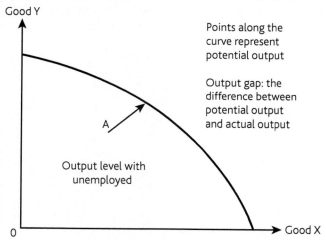

Figure10.7 *Cost of unemployment*

Inefficient allocation of government expenditure

Poverty results in a misallocation of government expenditure. Governments often have to implement a host of programmes aimed at alleviating and reducing poverty, such as transfer programmes, social safety nets and subsidies. Because government resources are finite, the opportunity cost incurred by such programmes include infrastructural development, which includes investments into road networks, improving highways, port systems and travel logistics, for example.

Social and environmental costs

Poverty is also associated with a host of social and environmental costs. Poverty has been shown to be associated with crime, illiteracy, innumeracy and the spread of certain diseases. Additionally, the poor often set up shanty town or slums on the outskirts of the urban centres. Such unplanned housing schemes lack proper sanitation systems as well as access to potable water, factors which can compound to have negative long-run effects on the environment.

Conclusion

This chapter explained the differences between the size and functional distribution of income. The concept of income inequality was also introduced. Discussions of the difference between absolute and relative poverty were proposed, as well as some of the factors contributing to poverty. Some of the measures to alleviate poverty were also discussed.

Key points

■ The size distribution of income refers to the distribution of income by individual, families and households.

■ The functional distribution of income or the factor share of income distribution refers to the distribution of income between the various factors of production.

■ The concept of inequality relates to the maldistribution of income across economic agents or across sectors.

■ Poverty refers to the condition of persons who lack adequate levels of income and wealth to access basic human needs, such as access to clean water, health care, nutrition, shelter and clothing.

End test

1   The supply curve of labour tends to be:
    a upward sloping   c horizontal
    b downward sloping   d backward bending

2   Why does the demand curve for labour slope downward?
    a the price of labour falls
    b the influence of diminishing marginal productivity
    c the law of diminishing marginal utility
    d imperfect competition

3   Amartya can choose between two plots of land to begin farming. If he chooses the plot on the eastern side, he will be able to produce $100,000 worth of tomatoes, maximising his profits. The economic rent for the eastern field is estimated at $10,000. If he chooses the plot on the western side, he can produce $150,000 worth of tomatoes with the same labour. How much rent will Amartya be willing to pay for the western plot?
    a $60,000   c $40,000
    b $50,000   d $30,000

4   Which of the following combinations include the four factors of production?
    a land, rent, interest and capital
    b rent, interest, capital and profits
    c entrepreneur, land, labour and capital
    d land, rent, wages and labour

5   Which of the following combinations include the rewards for each of the four factors of production?
    a land, rent, interest and capital   c entrepreneur, land, labour and capital
    b rent, interest, capital and profits   d land, rent, wages and labour

6 What is one possible explanation for the existence of wage differentials between workers in the same industry?

    a level of education

    b experience and age

    c skill and training

    d all of the above

7 How is the Gini coefficient defined?

    a a measure of income inequality

    b a measure of rent

    c a measure of profits

    d a measure of the economic transfers

8 How is the Lorenz curve defined?

    a a measure of rent

    b a measure of profits

    c a measure of income inequality

    d a measure of the economic transfers

9 Which of the following best defines the term 'compensating differentials'?

    a higher salaries for workers who face high levels of risks

    b senior citizens pension grant

    c compensation paid to new workers

    d medical benefits paid for all workers

10 Which of the following is not an economic cost of poverty?

    a unemployed human resources

    b inefficient allocation of government expenditure

    c social and environmental costs

    d increased productivity

End test feedback

1 d backward bending

2 b the influence of diminishing marginal productivity

3 a $60,000

4 c entrepreneur, land, labour and capital

5 b rent, interest, capital and profits

6 d all of the above

7 a a measure of income inequality

8 c a measure of income inequality

9 a higher salaries for workers who face high levels of risks

10 d increased productivity

Tutor-marked assignment

1 In the context of the production function, who are entrepreneurs?

2 Explain the term 'derived demand'.

3 Briefly explain the theory of distribution.

4 How is the marginal productivity of land calculated?

5 What does 'capital' entail?

6 Define the term 'wage differentials'. What factors contribute to wage differentials?

7 Briefly explain how trade unions intervene to determine wages.

8 Distinguish between the size and functional distribution of income.

9 How would an economy measure income inequality?

10 List three economic costs of poverty.

Feedback

1 Entrepreneurs initiate businesses and develop clever ways of producing and distributing goods. They seize opportunities in the market by investing and taking risks.

2 The term 'derived demand' is often used to refer to the demand for factors of production given that factors of production are demanded as an input into a production process.

3 The theory of distribution focuses on providing the tools of analysis to understand the various factor markets.

4 Using the general formula, the marginal productivity of land can be determined as

$$MP_{Land} = \frac{\Delta Output}{\Delta Land}$$

5 Capital refers to the man-made contributions to the production of goods and services.

6 Wage differentials can be defined as the difference in wage rates between two classes of workers. Wage differentials can be attributed to a host of factors including differences in skills and formal qualifications, experience and training, whether or not labour is unionised, and the age of workers; consider that wage differentials can exist in the teaching profession.

7 Trade unions can influence wages via collective bargaining. Collective bargaining refers to the process by which workers unite to negotiate wages and other working conditions with employers.

8 The size distribution of income refers to the distribution of income by individuals, families and households. In other words, it relates to income distribution among economic agents. The size distribution of income is the most common form of measuring income distribution. The functional distribution of income or the factor share of income distribution refers to the distribution of income between the various factors of production. The theory is concerned with measuring the share of wages, as compared to interest, wages and profits.

9 Income inequality can be measured using the Lorenz curve and the Gini coefficient.

10 Three economic costs of poverty, include:

   a unemployed human resources

   b inefficient allocation of government expenditure

   c social and environmental costs.